How to Get Even with the Universe
by
Getting Right with the World

Working within Sacred Space and Time

Steve Guettermann

Visit the author at: www.steveguettermann.com

Cover photo and design by Bruce Park.
Contact: brucio.artisto@gmail.com

Library of Congress Cataloging-in-Publication applied for.

ISBN: 0986093912
ISBN-13: 978-0986093913

Thank you, don Oscar ~ for the keys to the Alexandrian Library.

Table of Contents

Acknowledgements

First, I want to acknowledge, with heartfelt appreciation, the many timeless and timely gifts received, not only during writing this book, but throughout my life. If I could offer one gift, or convey one thing to others in return, it would be this: be forever in awe of the beauty and magic of this Planet. Aside from any alternate universe or numinous reality, the astounding life and consciousness on Planet Earth, which the Ascended Masters are said to call the Water Planet, boggles my mind with its creative potential and expression, as well as our joys for opportunity and wonder. I suggest we never cease to be in amazement with every step we take in the natural world.

There is wonder and magic all around. Simply imagining seeing our Planet from space shows its singular beauty and life. It is rare, if not unique, among the stars. Before we allow ourselves to be hell-bent on her destruction, let's step back and consider the possibility that what we can experience and learn here would fill countless lifetimes. To live in something other than awe is to deny our humanity and our possibility by placing ego and fear above what gives us life. In other words, physical life is beyond my creative powers to imagine. And yet here I am, so it seems.

Next I want to say thank you to some of the folks who helped me with this book. My heartfelt appreciation goes to Bruce Park, artist and friend extraordinaire, who contributed his time and talent to design the cover of this book. Bruce, along with his wife, and my friend, Genise, continue to help me explore the repertoire of the many ways of giving back to the Planet and people for their support.

I want to thank the good people who took time to review the manuscript that became this book before it was fit for public viewing. They compassionately guided me over its rough spots towards a smooth and succinct conveyance of how to get right with the world. I especially want to thank Judy Steele and Beth Walden for their tenacious and fervent scrutiny of this work, lest I remove it from the oven too soon, so to speak. A special thanks goes to doña Cindy Miro-Quesada, who brought completion of this work through right relationship.

I mention these three wise men in the book, alluding to some of the lessons they gave me: Jack Schwartz, Jim Miller and don Oscar Miro-Quesada. As I try to put *their* wisdom into action, and describe what

I've learned from them in my own words, their influence on me cannot be overestimated or over appreciated.

In a similar vein are those I often refer to as my "Sun Dance Family," the people with whom I've shared sweat lodges, vision quests, sun dances and other sacred, as well as secular, experiences. They include Skinnas Akayim and Joanne Smith, Alberta Iron Cloud, Ardis Iron Cloud, Ted Hamilton, Eric and Dana Boyd, Jay Ritter, Ken Hall, Tom Savage and family, Wade Miller, George Karl, Jeff Galuza, Mark Johnson, David and Cindi Iron Cloud, Kirby Smith, Jerry Dunson, Rod Cline, Anne Rockhold, Michael and Linda Gard, Robyn Bridges, Joe Lordi, Pieter Lefferts, Wendy West, Nurse Jeri Krenek, Yola Dunne, Andula Zach, Darcy DeTienne and Irina Shiyanovskaya. The friendship, laughs, food, suffering, wonderings and wanderings we continue to share are a soul-soothing elixir.

To Victoria and Dano, I must say the love you give me is beyond any other blessing.

And finally to Deborah ~ *wopila tanka pour rêver tant du rêve avec moi.*

I love you all!

Haylli!

"Life is much too important to be taken seriously."
Oscar Wilde

FOREWORD

Humanly written, with humility and humor in equal measure, *How to Get Even with the Universe by Getting Right with the World: Working within Sacred Space and Time* is an enchantingly eloquent unveiling of hands-on perennial wisdom, earth honoring ceremonial artistry and soul restorative personal revelation. Lovingly gestated into being within the infinitely fertile empyrean womb of my shamanic soul brother and treasured friend *Corazón Pensante*, (Thinking Heart) aka Steve Guettermann, I'm certain the living truth encountered within the pages of this remarkable book will undoubtedly prove to be a classic in the field of neo-shamanic earth literacy and contemporary ethnospiritual inquiry. Not only is Steve's gift of storytelling on a par with the soul illuminating tales spoken by tribal wisdom keepers of time immemorial, his honestly transparent narrative style invites us to gain deeper insight into our personal struggles and existential challenges as vital preparation for walking more gently and lovingly as sacred passersby upon our Earth Mother, Gaia-Pachamama. A rare gift of inspirational word, illuminating vision and cross-cultural shamanic ritual practice, *How to Get Even with the Universe by Getting Right with the World: Working within Sacred Space and Time* is a beacon of hope for all people called to embody a beauty walk of eco-spiritual healing presence upon beloved Pachamama.

Walking in beauty is being conscious of the sacred reciprocity governing All Our Relations, deeply aware of the exquisite balance between what is taken and what is given during our passerby journey upon this good earth. This unconditional act of generosity, of freely giving without regard for receiving anything in return, embodies the indigenous ethos, the core cultural identity that has guided the lives of our traditional earth honoring peoples before the advent of recorded history. Known as *ayni* by Quechua speaking peoples of Heart Island (South America), it is widely embraced as "cosmic or universal common sense," having become an inviolate principle of right living that informs and governs every human affair and activity in a manner sustaining of deep reverence for our Originating Mystery and Great Sacred Web of Life as a whole. An authentic life of *ayni* demands visceral attentiveness to the pulses, rhythms, cycles, and perpetual ebb and flow among all things born of Creation's dreaming. A life of *ayni* is labor of unconditional love, a soul restorative shamanic path through which our thoughts and visionary dreams, words and medicine songs, actions and gratitude dances, all find seven generation eco-spiritual sanctification in the world.

The greatest gift we humans have to offer the earth is our heartfelt appreciation for the blessing that is life. This experience of gratitude carries a quality of engagement and belongingness within it, of bringing ourselves into alignment with the rest of creation. Anytime gratitude is felt and given expression we become conscious co-creators in the unfolding journey of life. Aligned with the powers of the universe we learn to serve the greatest good for All Our Relations. In this manner expressing gratitude becomes an act of creative confidence, for emptied of the needs of our ego personality we free ourselves to come into deeply caring relationship with the whole of Creation. In essence, within our human impulse to gratitude flow the vast cycles of universal reciprocity. Through our loving recognition, the rest of the Earth achieves a deep fulfillment. Our praise and thanksgiving are as essential a part of life's "give and take," as are the cycles of oxygen and water or any other nourishment flowing through the biosphere. For everything that is taken, something has to be given in return. Life is give and take and all prayerful expressions of gratitude involve a reverent sense of belonging. Among native Quechua speaking people of Perú when we say *Yusulpayki* – or thank you – we are really saying "we belong together," we acknowledge our interdependence, meaning that we *all* belong together, that we are of each other. We belong here. Life belongs here. Belonging is the basic truth of our existence. In its deepest sense, at the heart of gratefulness, we also find this expression of reciprocal belonging known as *Living in Ayni* when we are freed from self-preoccupation and can be filled with thankful reverence for the sacrosanct gift that is life.

As *How to Get Even with the Universe by Getting Right with the World: Working within Sacred Space and Time* movingly reminds us WE ARE the Earth. Pachamama-Gaia shapes us, as we shape her; she informs our body and inhabits our soul, for what surrounds us, is us – the air we breath, the water we drink, the food we eat, is as much in us as it is of the living Earth. To live a sustainable life of harmony and balanced reciprocity with All Our Relations – mineral, plant, animal and human, seen or unseen – we must prayerfully dedicate our dreams, thoughts, words and actions to the wellbeing of the entire earth community. To fully live this understanding is to follow our Original Instructions and engage in the Great Work of restoring a soul animated experience of the sacred to the world. It requires us to stop, to feel, to listen, ever more deeply, to the sanctified inhalation and exhalation of Mother Earth's breathing, to the resonant drum beat of her perennial wisdom heart and soul sentience. Within the pages of this book, we are treated to a refreshingly incisive marriage of personal revelation and time honored ceremonial artistry. It is a body of work that inspires and catalyzes our human awareness of the accessible magic at play behind Creation's dreaming our world into form. Its embodied vision serves as a beautifying gift for the human soul, an opening and passageway beyond our current obsession with materiality.

The indigenous soul exists in all of us – we are all native children born from the miracle that is Gaia-Pachamama's dreaming. All traditional earth honoring people living today are very closely tied to critical habitat and biodiversity hotspots. They are the stewards not only of habitat, but most important, of the indigenous soul to which we are all heir and which we must reclaim. Laying aside our anger about the past and our fear of the future, both indigenous and non-indigenous people must exercise a spiritually compassionate activism as our healing legacy to the seven generations. It takes the ability to be fully alive to the present and let that earthy song come through us. In doing so, we inhabit not only the land, but the ground of our Being, where past and future fall away and we are enlightened fully, as the soul of the planet. Most earth honoring traditional people wisely proclaim that the future is behind us and that we are really moving towards the past, just as a plant during all its phases of outward growth is in reality moving toward the seed from which it originated. Or, to paraphrase Australian aboriginal elder Banjo Clarke: "Life is a *walk about* of return to our original Dreaming." The reality is that there is no "environment," save in our imaginations. Drawing from diverse sources of earth honoring shamanic medicine ways and ritual practices, we must inspire each other to walk a graceful path of healing beauty upon our beloved Pachamama, celebrating life as a sacred gift, and teaching Love by the way we live. This is my understanding of the Original Instructions bestowed upon humankind by Originating Mystery.

How to Get Even with the Universe by Getting Right with the World: Working within Sacred Space and Time, is a living embodiment of these Original Instructions. It is about living in *ayni*, about living in beauty, about a divinely ordained balanced reciprocity between what is freely received and generously offered forth to serve a healthful thriving of our species-wide interdependent relationship as Pachamama's children. It is a compelling invitation for humankind to embark upon a journey of inspired evolution and enlightened right action – to reclaim a soul animated time of dreaming the world into form, a prophesied time of human shamanic presence when we again shall move through a wilderness where every plant, every rock, every animal speaks to us, each embracing us in its song. For this I say *Yusulpayki*, my beloved brother, Steve, *yusulpayki!*

Don Oscar Miro-Quesada
Joshua Tree ~ January 16, 2017

1

Mystery Loves Company

"What you call science, I call magic. What you call magic, I call science."
Jim Miller – Lakota spiritual leader, describing a cultural difference

Giving back is life's most important principle for many traditional cultures. Although elaborate ceremonies have their place, this book provides a simple framework for engaging the world in more refined ways by creating and using sacred space, sacred reciprocity, authenticity and the possibilities they may create. These are things anyone can do alone or with others. Sacred reciprocity is known by Peruvian shamans as *ayni*, pronounced eye-knee. Ayni encourages us to become more in tune with the planet and the changes in us as we ritually acknowledge what we receive. This book invites your own experience of *soulular* growth through sacred reciprocity, and it offers ways to create and hold sacred space in which to give back. More than anything, ayni fosters right relationship between us and the seen and unseen worlds in order to maintain life. It's simple, actually. When we give back to that which supports us, it responds with something more than subsistence in return. That something more is magic.

What is magic? It is the home field advantage. Magic is the amazing, the inexplicable, joy, love, compassion, timing, synchronicity and patience. Magic is omnipresent. Magic is everything that sustains us. It is life, death, love, the coming and going of souls and spirits, and the changing passage of time, when it moves fast and when it moves slowly. Magic is miraculous healings, brought about by re-establishing right relationship. Magic is wonder. It is water. It is wisdom. Magic is what we cannot understand. Magic is what we can understand. Magic is the continuous flow and connectivity of the spontaneous omnipresent. Once we know that magic is everywhere and in everything, we begin to trust it and we begin to trust our ability to direct it because we are magic, too. Magic is what gives the hero's snowball a chance in hell. This book offers ways to recognize it, honor it, use it and say thank you.

When we approach our world through ayni, we expand possibility. My intent is to help the reader new to a spiritual path make sense of the basics of creating sacred space. It may also help the more advanced teacher or student guide others into creating that space. Although some concepts may be familiar, I will strive to put them in a new light so they have new application. On the other hand, a new idea may require a re-reading or two, but practice will help even more. There are practices and exercises at the end of several chapters for you to test the validity of what is presented. I suggest you stay open to new revelations your experiences and intuition bring you. Those will serve you much better than anything you read. The truth won't set you free, but your truth will.

How does ayni differ from other forms of saying thank you? It is really a celebration of appreciation and often takes place as a ceremony within sacred space. We give something back to the planet we have received or created ourselves. When this is done consistently within the context of sacred space, it becomes a highly vibrational relationship-shifting exchange that alters our awareness and behavior.

Here's a short story as an example.

KIM

It takes days of hard work to get the grounds ready for a Sun Dance, a prayer ceremony of many North American Plains tribes. There is a lot of good food and company, too. Sweat lodges are built, the arbor in which the Sun Dance takes place is built or repaired, the land is cleaned up, firewood is cut, sweat rocks gathered, tipis put up, last year's Sun Dance Tree is dug out and cut up and the hole readied for the new one. There's usually an *inipi* – sweat lodge ceremony – each night after the day's work is done, too. When all is ready, the new Sacred Tree is sanctified, ceremoniously cut down the day before Sun Dance starts, loaded onto the shoulders of the men and brought into the arbor. The hole for the tree is prayed over and fed sacred food. The dancers tie their ropes and offerings onto the tree. Then the supporters tie on their offerings. Finally the tree is slid into the hole and raised. When I danced, I couldn't wait to start the Sun Dance, praying it would be easier than getting ready for it.

Sometimes it was. Sometimes it wasn't.

In my experience, the Sun Dance season starts at the summer solstice and runs for about seven weeks. The four day Sun Dance is a time of renewal for dancers and supporters, a time of prayer and vows, a time of release and receiving. It's also a time of great thanks. And it's almost always hot. (One year there was a Sun Dance north of Calgary, Alberta, Canada when we danced in freezing rain, but that was unusual. It's still known as the Ice Dance.) Dancers don't eat during the four days; we usually got water at night after we came out of the sweat lodge. Some don't even get that. We sweat in the morning before the sun comes up. Then dance. Then sweat after the sun goes down.

It was really hot one year. During a late afternoon break, a supporter sent in a bottle of very nice organic aloe vera lotion. There were maybe 30 dancers who shared it. When I got it the first time, it was slightly over half full. When I got it the second time, it was slightly over half full. When I got it the third time, it was slightly over half full. I couldn't believe it. I squeezed a bunch in my hand to see what would happen. When I turned the bottle upright, it was still slightly over half full.

"Another Sun Dance miracle," I thought.

Does an endless bottle of aloe have practical application? When the summer sun baked us like cookies and rocks glowed red hot in the fire for the sweat lodge that we'd have later, yes, an endless bottle of aloe has endless practical application. And that is magic.

After the Sun Dance I tried to find who sent the aloe in. Organic aloe vera doesn't just show up by itself...or does it?

My girlfriend said, "Oh, Kim sent that in."

That made perfect sense. Kim was likely one of the sweetest people on earth and the wife of a very good friend of mine, another dancer.

It was tough when Kim passed. She was so authentic, happy, kind and generous. I can see her smile and hear her laugh as I write this. She and my girlfriend were best friends. In time, my girlfriend and I went into the mountains near where Kim and her husband had lived as ranch caretakers to do a ceremony for Kim a few months after she passed. She had a lock of Kim's hair and wanted to release it into the creek where all of us used to go together. As we said prayers, a whirlwind kicked up. It circled around through the trees, crossed over the creek, and then whirled around where the two of us sat and settled on us, whirling without moving on. But this whirlwind didn't carry dust. All it carried were open cottony seedpods from the cottonwood trees. We were positively smothered with little downy puffball-like kisses, especially the ones that hit our faces. The whirlwind spun around us with thousands, maybe tens of thousands of kisses, and then slowly stopped. The seedpods settled onto the ground or floated away in the creek. We sat there quietly for the longest time.

We knew it was Kim. And I know that somewhere, that bottle of aloe is sitting behind the mirror in someone's medicine cabinet, still slightly over half full.

~~~~~~~~~~~~~~~~~~

These stories within-the-story told above suggest that the beauty and magic of sacred space can take many forms. When we show up with ayni, magic shows up. We'll get into this more, but sacred space is not so much a confine as it is a state of energy. It can be mobile, it can be fixed, but it is always conscious. Through ceremonial interactions with and within the three dimensional sacred space of physical reality, we can access the fourth dimension of sacred space/time and beyond. In these other dimensions there are new rules on top of the 3D rules. When these rules collide, they are often referred to as paradoxes. They can make us question what is really going on, and they should. We may find that old patterns don't work, but we can't explain or accept new ones. However, rather than experience a paradigm shift as an irreconcilable collision of confusion, we can choose a wiser path. That path allows new experiences and realities to build upon one another as we rebuild ourselves.

When we first enter sacred space and perceive it to be in a neutral and nascent form, anything can happen. Just as Thomas Edison finally used a neutral filament between a positive and negative charge to create a long lasting light bulb (rather than the rapid burnout he kept having) our initial neutral, receptive presence can yield an enlightened re-
~~~~~~~~~~~~~~~~~~

sponse in harmony with the dynamic positive masculine and negative feminine energies of sacred space. A positive masculine energy simply means energy that gives form, and a negative feminine energy is a releasing or outward expressing energy. Both are necessary to sustain form. One is not better than the other. These energies are part of the beauty of sacred space that beckon us to explore the interplay of infinite possibility. And what about that neutral filament? Metaphorically, it represents our role as the true maestro of sacred space. How we orchestrate these different energies can create and maintain a space that serves us, others and the planet for the highest and greatest good of all. This is the essence of sacred reciprocity. It's a gift to give back in such a way.

Evidence suggests that the first musical instruments after the human voice were percussion instruments. People made music beating on a log, for example. Then came flutes. True drums followed about 37,000 years ago, as people learned to stretch animal hides over a frame. After all that time, there is no end in sight or sound to the potential music that can come from a drum or flute. Even as a beginner, the never-before-heard music we can make with a drum or a flute is inexhaustible. Now imagine we learn to play a piano and our skill progresses from chopsticks to Chopin. Even as a concert pianist we still haven't dented all that is possible. The point is, whether we know a little or a lot, there is no limit to what we can do or experience.

Sacred space is the same. We do not need to know much to attract endless magic from our relationship with sacred space and reciprocity. Magic shows up when we do. But as we get more skilled, we have more fun. We can also attract a larger orchestra. In regards to sacred space, this means we attract beneficent spirit guides and allies. Thus whether our offerings emulate beating on a log or the music of the spheres, when we give back with a good heart, denizens of both seen and unseen realms will sit with us, listen and applaud.

Mother Earth, Gaia (Greek), Pachamama (Quechua), Maca Unci (Lakota), all of these terms acknowledge our planet is a living and conscious being. A pervasive indigenous belief is, "Everything is always watching." This isn't meant in some creepy, perverted or Big Brother sort or way, but from the perspective that everything, including stones, plants and animals, has some degree of awareness. If we had no awareness of being received by something other than ourselves, there would be no sense in giving offerings and attempting to connect with something other than ourselves. For our offerings to be received, obviously something outside of us must be aware and sentient. Seen and unseen worlds hold individuals and individual energies, combined into an interactive web of omni-responding consciousnesses of multiple generations and dimensions.[1] Ayni helps us become sensitive to them and creates a greater sense of self and a greater understanding of self through our connection to the whole. Some people call this nature. Some call it the web of life. Some call it creation.

We live in a universal ocean of energy where both opposites and likes attract. Our happiness, fulfillment, expression and health depend upon how we use this energy and give it form. They also depend on how we transform and shapeshift that which has form. Transformation is magic, too. The task is to live within the parameters of physical and non-physical realities, and create our own reality from them. For example, it makes no difference whether the glass is half empty or half full. What matters is we drink and we enjoy, knowing that whatever filled the glass in the first place can refill it again. Ayni triggers the refill because it brings balance. Apparently ayni also works for aloe.

This book is not for the scientist, the believer or nonbeliever. It is for the *imaginator* who questions, observes and does something with questions and observations. While it is true that ayni leads to and yields magic, there are even more benefits. Sacred reciprocity leads to joy and purpose, belonging and connection, laughter and amusement, and is an antidote to feeling adrift and powerless. It restores beauty and grace, which is our natural movement within the sea of seen and unseen realms. It elevates and shapeshifts giving back into a sacred relationship of connection with all that is. Not only does everything see us; everything hears us. Once we begin to hear the universe and life, what may be their infrequent whispers become louder messages and the signs become clearer. So you will likely hear voices in your head. Is this a sign you are going crazy? I don't know, but I do agree with don Oscar Miro-Quesada who says, "First you have to lose your mind in order to come to your senses."

---

[1] Geobiologist Yann Lipnick has developed a thorough classification system of subtle and spiritual life forms based on his observations. He teaches his techniques to others with a good degree of success. Most of his work is in French, but there are English translations of two of his books available from iTunes.

Or we can say, "Oh, what a web we weave when we first practice to receive." The web is spun when we consciously, sincerely, ritualistically and happily give back in honest appreciation to the magical forces that influence our life. Ayni helps us connect, whether it be with a sparrow, a stream spirit, a mountain deity, our higher self, other people, guardian angels, power animals, a blessed virgin, god, or the god or goddess within. There is only one thing we have to gain and only one thing we have to lose by learning the ways of magic. Everything.

2

Good Medicine

"The greater the scientist, the more he is impressed with his ignorance of reality, and the more he realizes that his laws and labels, descriptions and definitions, are the products of his own thought. They help him to use the world for purposes of his own devising rather than understand and explain it."
Alan Watts – The Wisdom of Insecurity

The Law of Attraction gets a lot of coverage these days, so I won't add much. I feel ayni provides more encompassing answers to life's more ponderous questions. It encompasses attraction, gratitude and more, including a shapeshifting of vibratory consciousness, which is key to spiritual evolution. However, for a better understanding later, I will highlight a few related concepts.

Manifesting energies are subtle. Science had, and still has to a large extent, a "Yes, but..." relationship to them. For example, on one hand science confirms that our bodies are electromagnetic and send emotionally charged energy into the environment. On the other hand, science says that force is too meager to have any real impact on anything because it quickly dissipates and is overwhelmed by stronger forces, such as electromagnetic interference in buildings. The dissipation is attributed to the Law of Inverse Squares.

In terms of both light and an electric field, the Law of Inverse

Squares states that an electric field twice as far from the source is spread over four times the area, hence it has one-fourth the intensity. This also applies to sound, gravity and radiation. So those who quickly dismiss the impact of ayni, magic, intent, prayer, the Law of Attraction and related phenomena use this law to override intended manifestation being possible because, according to the Law of Inverse Squares, any such field would quickly dissipate. Yet science cannot refute that every single thing man has created was first a thought. Anecdotally, this can be tested with help from that old song, "When You're Smiling, the Whole World Smiles With You" by Louis Armstrong. In other words, it's easy to impact reality. It seems that although we may not fully understand how reality works, holding on to laws and beliefs that don't hold up should not hold us back. Even that practical and imaginative wizard scientist, Albert Einstein, acknowledged what he called "spooky action at a distance," despite the fact he could not get himself to fully believe that energy particles separated by large distances could share information. But they do, as quantum physics confirms, although not all scientists accept this.

Consequently, it seems wise to seek environments that are complementary to our vibration so our web of influence is greater and more easily manifested. In a complementary environment, our energy won't dissipate so quickly. And, once we reach that energetic integration where we and the environment resonate together, then there is no difference between the sources – the outer source and the inner source resonate in harmony – creating a creative connection. Don Oscar refers to something similar as, "Creativity creating creation," which is a beautiful corollary to spooky action at a distance.

Let's go a little deeper. A double-blind study is a study in which both the investigator and the participant are blind to, or unaware of, the nature of the treatment the participant is receiving. Double-blind trials are thought to produce objective results, since the expectations of the researcher and the participant about the experimental treatment do not affect the outcome. Triple-blind studies are common, too, in which data collectors do not have enough information to impact the research. Blind studies are used to eliminate researcher or subject bias, be it intentional or unconscious. Consequently, researchers are very occupied with assuring intent does not adulterate experiments. Their actions support the idea, or fear, that intent is a force to be reckoned with. So while double and triple blind experiments guard against the possibility that experiments can be manipulated by the conscious or unconscious bias of researchers and subjects, the Law of Inverse Squares "confirms" intent is not strong enough to have any real impact.

Wow. Imagine that. Although unconscious bias may influence scientific results, science won't acknowledge that conscious intention influences reality. No wonder laughter is good medicine. The double talk is hilarious.

But there is even more to it than that. One of the most profound scientific discoveries of the last millennium occurred in 1999. Basically, through repeatable experiments, it was scientifically validated that the answer to the question, "Is the observer effect real?" is an unequivocal "Yes." This means it has been documented that the person who observes scientific experiments impacts the results. This is known as Bell's Theorem. In other words, all of us impact reality. Quantum physicists, theoretical physicist Stephen Hawking, the Dalai Lama, Louis Armstrong and many others agree. When we use this power within sacred space, we can have far reaching and multi-dimensional impacts.

3

In the beginning…

"Let the water ground you."
Thoth

My first time in a sweat lodge I was with a Lakota named Wallace Black Elk and about fifteen other people. As we sat quietly in the dark, Wallace said, "When you come in here, you are in kindergarten." I immediately thought, 'Aw, c'mon, Wallace. I'm at least in first grade." I thought I was that spiritually advanced. He kept talking as the hot, red-orange glowing lava rocks were brought in. The lodge warmed up, but I did not understand real heat until the lodge was closed and Wallace poured water on the rocks and steam hit my body. I remember thinking, "Oh, my god. This is what they are talking about!" The native people sang, but I couldn't breathe. I thought the skin would blister off my back. How could he do this to a first grader?

I now realize Wallace was being kind when he said we were in kindergarten. These days I don't feel I've passed pre-school. And for that, I am eternally grateful to him. There is so much to learn.

The world is very kind to me, too, to absorb my delinquency and truancy, for I've been less than a dedicated learner of the mysteries and possibilities so generously offered me. It's taken me years and many sweats to begin to understand the *ceremony* of the sweat lodge, the *inipi*, which means breath of life. This book is not about the *inipi* either, but it is about sacred space, which spiritual ceremony enlivens.

Around the same time I met Wallace, I met Jack Schwarz. I write about Jack a bit later, so won't say much about him now other than he was highly revered as an intuitive and psychic by his students, whom he amazed, and by scientists who studied him. I will share my first meeting with him now, though.

My good friend and business partner, Sandy, with whom I owned and operated a martial arts studio, saw Jack one night at one of Jack's public lectures. Sandy called me the next day and said, "I met don Juan!"

I thought, 'What the hell?'

Sandy said Jack Schwarz was like don Juan, of Carlos Castaneda fame, and Sandy wanted me to go with him to Jack's lecture that night and take Jack out for coffee. According to Sandy, Jack wowed the audience the night before with his perceptions of people's energy fields and Sandy knew he had found a "real McCoy" at last. I didn't think there was a chance of Jack going for coffee with us, but Sandy and I went to the lecture. This was a few days after I had a rare telephone call with one of my sisters, who really wanted to know why I lived as I did. I was somewhat reclusive at the time.

To my surprise, Jack and his wife had coffee with Sandy and me that night. Sandy and Jack did most of the talking, but then Jack turned to me and said in his thick Dutch accent, "Vell, Steve, you don't say much, but I can see there's a lot going on there. As a matter of fact, I would say you like trees better than you like people."

I looked at him aghast. He gave me an amused look I would come to know well. That was exactly word-for-word what I had told my sister on the phone several days earlier, not the type of thing one says in casual conversation. Jack had my attention from then on and with good reason. Over the years I watched him continually baffle people with his abilities to perceive intricacies of their energy field, without ever indulging intimacies. He didn't say general things that would apply to just anyone. There was a lot of "you like trees better than people" specific stuff. I also saw him demonstrate his own ability to rapidly heal himself. His demonstrations and explanations taught me a lot.

Sandy and I both studied and worked with Jack at his Health, Education and Research Training – H.E.A.R.T. – Center near Ashland, Oregon. I also co-authored one of Jack's books titled *It's not what you eat, but what eats you!*

But my heart clamored for Montana, so I left Oregon and ultimately settled in Bozeman. Montana was losing population at the time. I had no idea that meant the economy was in the toilet. I was unfazed. I told myself, "I can write. I can teach. I can work construction." I had no idea I would have to do all three at the same time. I consistently worked 60 to 80 hours a week. I was a spiritual being having a financial collapse. It stressed a weak marriage that ultimately dissolved. There was no sacred space. No getting right with the world. And no getting right with each other.

1999 was a rough year. Despondent over my divorce, likely more due to ego than lost love, I had also lost my job when the herbal company of which I was general manager sold, and I broke my back on Valentine's Day doing squats. I was down and drinking heavily again. I needed something to move me in the right direction. In June, friends got me in touch with Jim Miller, a Lakota spiritual leader from Porcupine, South Dakota. He invited me to participate in a *hanbleceya*, a vision quest. After several years of going on the hill, as it's also known, I began to Sun Dance with Jim and others. I danced for seven years and assisted for at least four more, at which time I felt my commitment was complete.

Some people have amazing experiences on the hill or during Sun Dance. To be struck by lightning is among the most profound. This is an honor, a sign of acceptance by the Thunder Beings for a special role. There is evidence some indigenous people harnessed lightning, directing it into the earth to fertilize the soil and to create atmospheric conditions conducive to health. They knew how to create all they needed from a union of the earth and sky. Ceremony teaches us to develop this union in physical and nonphysical ways.

I haven't been hit by lightning yet, but I saw and heard spirits, heard native children laughing who lived at least a hundred years ago, and witnessed the screams and destruction of an Indian village of which I was a part when soldiers attacked it. These may be interesting, but the real thing is how ceremony begins to infiltrate day-to-day behavior.

First, it is important to understand that Jim Miller was not always a spiritual leader. A product of the reservation system and Indian boarding schools, Jim experienced physical abuse, sexual abuse, drug abuse and cultural depredations. A decorated Vietnam Combat veteran, he also was in the federal prison system after being captured by U.S. Marshals following a shootout at Wounded Knee in 1973. His story has evolved from hate, anger, pain, addiction, violence and hopelessness to love and compassion. The risks he took to open his ceremonies to all people are evidence that he truly walks the Red Road: the road of consciousness and strength. His experiences shaped mine through reconciliation with others, as well as with my own heart.

In my first sweat with Jim, he gave those of us who would go on the hill instructions on how to prepare. The preparations included getting materials needed for the *hochoka*, the sacred altar space. These preparations protect a person when on hanbleceya. I needed to understand I was going before forces and spirits normally not sensed during daily Western life. Being exposed in such a way during days of fasting and prayer calls these powers in. Just exactly what they may do, one never knows. Hence, one must prepare for anything. Jim runs hot sweat lodges, too. That did not dissuade me, so after the lodge, I went home and got ready to go on the hill.

A week later, we met Jim for another lodge right before we went up. It was even hotter. Knowing I would be without water for up to four days made me more attached to the sweat flowing from my pores. Jim said someone would get us when it was time to come down, and we'd go back into the lodge for another purification. There, we'd say whatever we wanted, then have a meal and a shower.

I soon realized how much support we receive in ceremony. The support – which is the energetic support of a greater collective, connected consciousness – came through family supporters, spirits, sights, sounds, feelings, dreams and perceptions. Despite the support, I suffered. I spent hours kneeling in my hochoka with my face to the ground. There were moments of pure bliss, too. Moonlight. Starlight. Incredible peace. One night I was kept company by the most beautiful bird sounds I'd ever heard. When Jim came to get us, I asked him what kind they were.

He shook his head in disbelief and quietly said, "Birds."

'Ohhhhh,' I thought to myself as the light came on, 'they were spirits.'

My hardest hanbleceya was when I was alone on the west face of the Bridger Mountains in Montana in July 2010. I had some shade, but it was really hot. It was the only vision quest during which I did not recover during the night. What made matters worse was that my hochoka was above a cool mountain stream I heard below. Thirst was truly maddening.

Why do this? To show the spirits we are serious about the vows we make, whether they are for us personally, for loved ones or for something else. Basically, we ask for two things: help and health. Engaging in ceremony can bring about the space and conscious action more conducive to fulfilling such requests and living our life's purpose. Central to all of this is the ceremonial space in which we offer heartfelt and heartful gratitude for what we have received to be where we are at that moment in time and space.

Enter don Oscar Miro-Quesada. Don Oscar is a Peruvian shaman and so much more. I first heard don Oscar speak during a webinar with Barbara Marx Hubbard in 2012 and thought, 'He seems authentic.' Consequently, my antennae were strongly activated, to discern if he was what he seemed to be. When I heard don Oscar was going to do an online shaman course, I thought, 'Oh, no. Not you, too.' I was dismayed he would disseminate his knowledge that way. But I soon had another thought. 'Well, if anything is going to be transmitted through the online ethers, it may as well be shamanism.' So, I enrolled. Later don Oscar expressed the same misgivings about teaching online, and then had the same change of heart, so to speak. Although I immediately accepted his information, I still was not sure about the man. I have authority issues.

The real test came the first time don Oscar and I met face to face at a retreat he offered to about fifty other people. It was well over a year after my initial virtual encounter with him. I still wasn't sure if he was all he seemed. Early one morning I went into our altar room without anyone there. I had no preconception or thought. I just wanted to be there alone. Once inside, I was encompassed by the most embracing, compassionate energy, coming from everyone's personal altars, as well as don Oscar's altars.

'This is real,' I thought. 'This can't be faked.' I felt sacred space before, but never like that.

Things got more real. Late one evening, don Oscar led us on a shamanic journey of death and rebirth. I soon was joined by one of my animal allies ~ a cougar. I became one, too. We ran together through the night desert. Once we stopped at a frozen waterhole. I saw our images reflected in the ice. We scratched it up with our claws. Then I was on my own. I ran. And I killed. I killed every animal I came across. I ran them down. I ambushed them from the trees. Every kill was like catnip on steroids to me. I reveled in knowing everything was afraid of and ran from me. Consumed by and confident in my power I attacked a grizzly bear. I jumped on his back. I hooked my claws into his muscles and sunk my teeth into his neck so deeply I felt his fur in the back of my throat. Retractable claws have to be one of the greatest adaptations in nature. Then a funny thing happened. He killed me so fast I have no idea how he did it. He buried me under a pile of leaves and loose dirt. I was dead. Deader than dead. Nothing. I completely decomposed into a void.

At some point I heard don Oscar's voice telling us to come back. I didn't want to. Somehow I reassumed my human form and became aware of lying on the floor. I finally sat up. Each person in the room seemed to be in a various state of return. What eventually brought me back to full consciousness were really stinky feet. The smell came from the man sitting to my left. I wondered why I didn't notice it before. I discreetly leaned toward him, only to find the smell was not coming from his feet. It was coming from the woman on my right and getting worse. I leaned toward her to make sure I had found the offender, but no, the smell wasn't coming from her either. I looked down at my feet. 'No!' I thought. As I bent over to check mine out, my nose passed over my cougar tooth necklace. That was it! I had decomposed so completely my cougar tooth necklace smelled rotten. I had to get out of there. I went to my room as quickly as possible.

The smell was nasty. My chest reeked, so maybe it came from the inside of me. I thought my heart had gone bad. I put Florida Water on the tooth and more on my chest, then showered. By morning the tooth was only faintly offensive, but I noticed some of the outer enamel was gone, which may be a testimony to the realness of the experience.

Thus began a more committed relationship to don Oscar and what it is I am supposed to do. For me, the lessons have come more from reflection rather than revelation. Voices or visions are not necessarily important. What is important is how the impact of ceremonial experience builds over time as one takes appropriate action. I have highlighted some of those impacts below. Each is offered more fully in subsequent pages and how they support a life of ayni and magic.

Appreciation – It is almost incomprehensible what thirst can do to a person and how good water can taste to someone almost dead from dehydration. Water is the best medicine. Nothing teaches appreciation like that first drink of water after days without it. Nothing. As I learn to appreciate everything like that first drink of water, I realize how much I am given each day. It took me years to understand that sitting on the hill in peaceful contemplation and appreciation is perhaps more important than asking for something.

Humility – After a few minutes in a sweat lodge with Wallace or Jim, it was impossible to feel I was better than anything else. If I could have breathed I would have screamed for mercy. Self-importance has no place in the abode of spirits, which means it has no place in daily life.

Compassion – Compassion never goes out of style. Compassion is not weakness. It is not stupidity. Frequently it simply entails choosing love over fear, kindness over arrogance, respect over neglect. Compassion comes from strength. Thus, true compassion simply cannot make the recipient of another's compassion dependent upon it. In other words, compassion strengthens both the giver and receiver. We may fear compassion because we fear making a person dependent upon us. The fact is, sometimes a handout is exactly what is needed. Unconditional compassion has a place. Be kind.

Being present – Being present makes a good teacher great and a great relationship terrific. The power of the moment of being totally present in space and time is so elusive, but it focuses and releases our power, which then becomes so inclusive. It keeps our energy from being siphoned off by distraction. Think of how you are when you are actively engaged with life in the moment. Being present leads us to...

Sacred Space – Spirits respond to sacred space. It begins in our heart. It extends into the world and beyond. I had no idea how important it is to create this until recently. Sacred space creates resonance with the unseen world of support and guidance. Creating, maintaining, sharing and carrying sacred space is one of the most important things I can do. It is the welcoming environment in which spirits come in and ask, "What do you want?" Sacred space is immanently connected to ceremony. Anyone can create ceremony and sacred space anywhere. It does not depend upon dogma or giving away one's power to be in the sacred space of another.

Shapeshifting – Everything shapeshifts. Shapeshifting is foundational to spiritual and shamanic practice. It is the constant motion and interplay of energy. It can be as easy as changing one's mind. When I change my relationship to a situation, I change the situation. Interacting with the world with the conscious intent of allowing it to shapeshift for the greatest good is high magic. Shapeshifting the body in a dream is an indication of growing personal power. Shapeshifting can carry over into physical life. People do shapeshift into animals. Shapeshifting also means allowing other people, especially those we love, to shapeshift into what they need to become. Often it requires letting go, which requires trust. Sustainability is not the goal. Shapeshifting is the goal. It is the change that creates the charge and the enhancement of the environment and sentient consciousness. Sustainability is an outcome of conscious shapeshifting. This means we get what we need when we allow change.

Giving and receiving – In the modern world, it is becoming harder to maintain the connection with what gives us life. Giving and receiving are types of shapeshifting. Shapeshifting is part of the natural order; squeezing things out of shape to survive is not. Right relationship acknowledges the connection of everything through the dynamic flow of interaction.

Surrender – Surrender but don't give your power away. Surrender is required, yet unique for each person. Going on the hill can break down one's resistance to whatever it is one is to accept in order to become what one is to be. Surrender is a source of true personal power. It is energy paradoxically created through simultaneous fusion and fission.

Intent – Life has power and purpose when one has intent and purpose. Intent shapeshifts the energy around us into the form we intend, up to a point. But intent never provides us with unfettered creation. We are connected to others, and thus impacted by the activities and creativities of others. For me, shapeshifting heart and mind, losing self-importance, and keeping my sense of humor are much more enjoyable ways of using intent compassionately, rather than trying to force something into existence that may cause more harm than good.

Paradox – The spiritual world opened up by a vision quest is a paradox. Nothing was as it seemed once I began to see things for what they could be, which is often more than I can imagine. Keener observation led me to understand I will never understand it all, while opening my world and senses to ever greater mystery and the appreciation of it. Paradox creates an enlivening sense of awe and wonder, trumping the boring world of a know-it-all kindergartener.

Science and Magic – Jim once said, "What you call science I call magic and what you call magic I call science." The cultural potential for misunderstanding is rife in this statement. Yet, quantum physics merges science and magic, both of which can be thought of as intended creation, into a compatible relationship of support rather than separation. I consider science and magic as the same side of the same coin. Intent is on the other.

Forgiveness – Forgiveness relieves karma and life presents a cornucopia of opportunities to make up for screw ups. One way things can work is that when we do not forgive, the energy of the past stays with us and needs to be balanced in some way. However, with true, heartfelt and unconditional forgiveness, there is no need for us to re-experience a path that someone else needs to get right.

For example, let's say you and your father had issues with each other. He provided a good home, but could not understand you so did his best to change you into something he could understand. You, on the other hand, simply wanted to be left alone and be you. Since that was not allowed, you rebelled in your own way...quietly, sullenly and surreptitiously. As you shut down, it became harder for you to express. As an adult, you attracted partners who also had an agenda for you. You being you was not on it. Consequently, those relationships did not last.

Years after your father's passing, you and he connected in meditation. From his current perspective, he could see he made some mistakes and basically asked if the two of you could do it again. Lovingly you said, "No," and forgave him for anything he should have known better and done better, but did not...maybe because of his fear and unwillingness to change. Still, that is no reason for you to relive another comparable experience, as you have moved beyond that. Perhaps later you will incarnate with a family that is at peace with itself, a family more in tune with your progression. In any case, through your forgiveness, your father is free to apply his new lessons of love and understanding in other ways and with other entities, as are you. And so, expression is manifested, karma is balanced and the souls' evolution continues.

4

Herding Cats

"Of all God's creatures, there is only one that cannot be made slave of the leash. That one is the cat. If man could be crossed with the cat it would improve the man, but it would deteriorate the cat."
Mark Twain

I have seven spirit cats that help me now: four cougar, a male and three females, two male jaguars and a female black panther. They have all come to me over time. The male cougar has been with me for years, even before I knew it. Cougar are also known as puma. Black panthers are jaguars. About 10% of jaguars are black.

It was during a vernal equinox sweat that Jaguar first showed up. I was in the lodge and first I saw the cougar pacing in the back, and then the jaguar. I thought I was being unfaithful to the cougar when the jaguar showed up. It's always interesting when such things happen as the lodge is pitch black, and then suddenly you see things in there. In any case, I thought "my" cougar would leave after the jaguar showed up, but he did not. So, I had two male cats. Then in late December of the following year, the black panther showed up in my house and was solidly with me in a tutelary animal lodge we had for the vernal equinox three months later. When none of this is spoken to anyone, and then other people tell you they see a panther in the lodge that is there for you – or wonder why I was sitting on a black panther – its obvious a panther is really in there.

There is another interesting thing about that spring tutelary animal lodge. I have a battery-operated Kit-Kat cat clock on the wall. Its eyes and tail rock back and forth at one second intervals. When the battery got weak, the movement stopped, but it still kept perfect time. I saw no reason to change the battery while the time was still good. The eyes and tail had not moved in nearly two months. The morning after the tutelary animal lodge, I was making the bed and heard a sound that caught my attention. I went to the kitchen. The clock's eyes and tail were going back and forth...almost as much as they did with a fresh battery. Coincidence? After all that cat energy in the lodge? I don't think so. It's something to accept and appreciate rather than understand.

With reciprocity and attentiveness, we can often discern what animal spirit guides one has. And guides may come and go as we or our needs change. So be attentive. When they show up, tell them your name. Ask them for theirs. Give them spirit food, which is just a little food offering. Animal spirit guides aren't pets, though. They are allies, helpers, but their affection can be profound. And when within sacred space, an ally may show up just for a moment to give you something of value, never to be heard from again.

We inherently know there are forces at work to which we acquiesce that provide unbelievable gifts and contacts. How many people say, "My dog found me," or "My cat picked me"? Once we realize our pets, our partners, our state of mind and everything else is a vibration, we can more easily understand that spirit allies and guides come to us out of the same sort of resonance. Many believe we have guardian angels. Why not guardian cats, dragons, snakes, turtles, unicorns or kangaroos?

There are several good animal spirit guidebooks available. *Animal Speak* by Ted Andrews is one. He offers ways to contact and nurture your animal guides. *Animal Spirit Guides* by Steven D. Farmer is another to check out. Another thing to realize is that animals that come to you in dreams or in waking reality may simply have a message for you. For example, say what you want about rabbits, but there are not a lot of them where I live. To see three of them in one day as I walked about my neighborhood was extraordinary. That night I checked one of my animal guidebooks to see what it had to say about rabbits. It was quite appropriate for the time and the moon. I saw another rabbit early the next day. I took it as an affirmation that what I read and surmised was accurate. In the following weeks, I saw only one. To me this means I got the right message.

Think of such encounters as subtext. Great Hollywood movies are replete with subtext, often defined as something like this: "an implicit undertone of conversation or action, which a character begins to understand as the production unfolds." Subtext keeps the audience from quickly becoming bored, which happens when everything is obvious. The magical world is a master of subtext. It's more fun that way.

When we give back through conscious ayni, we learn how to receive in ways that help the cycles of life and evolution continue in ways that serve the highest good. Reciprocity can even help us find a teacher, because anything can be a teacher: a person, a spirit, a plant, an animal, a moment, an observation, a rock, and often in extremely practical ways.

Cat's paw

Years before I shapeshifted into a cougar with don Oscar, I had been attuned to them. At one time I rented a place where "wild animals" were caged on the property. The animals included a male and female cougar in separate cages. The cages were no more than 120 square feet or so. After a while the animals got to know me, especially the male cougar. My understanding is that male cougars do not tolerate human males very well, but it was different between us. The eyes, ears and tail of a cat say a lot.

I can't remember how it started, but one day I was crouched at the cage and the cat was rubbing against my hand. He had a very deep purrrrr and obviously enjoyed the contact. I think even human company was a welcome respite from a wood plank floor and a boxed-in metal enclosure. So, I worked him over in a good way. I imagined what great shape he would have been in had he been wild. He had that square, powerful cougar head and was well muscled despite his confines.

As I prepared to stand, the look in his eye changed from don't stop to don't go! I spontaneously pulled my head back just as a forepaw zipped past the bars and tried to grab me behind the head. He was not trying to hurt me. He just did not want me to go. In the future I only got up to leave when he wasn't looking right at me. In any case, we both seemed to enjoy these encounters greatly. He was declawed, so often he'd put his paw in my hand and we'd pull on each other paw-to-hand in tug-o-war fashion.

On the day I moved out, I was at the river saying good-bye prayers. As I walked toward the house, I heard a scream. I ran toward the cages. The cat was on his back looking up at a guy kneeling on top of him. Then the guy smacked the cat in the face. I thought, 'You shouldn't have done that.' The cat whipped up off the ground and was on his hind legs in a flash as the guy backpedaled. He bit the guy on the forehead, ripping his head open. If the cat had claws, the guy would have been shredded. By then a second guy came out of his RV with a can of bear pepper spray. He sprayed both his friend and the cat. That broke off the attack. The guy ran out of the cage, nearly blind from the pepper spray and blood pouring from his head. His friend took him to the hospital.

I turned on a garden hose and began to gently wash the cat's face and head. He had been rubbing his face on the floor, trying to get the pepper out of his eyes. As I began to wash his face, I heard him purrrrr. It really broke my heart.

I moved out and did not go back for months. But I had permission to make a sacred pipe for ceremony and wanted to carve a cougar paw into the bowl. I wasn't quite sure how a cougar paw looked, so I went back to the property, hoping I could see the cat. He remembered me and we bonded again. I checked out his paws, needing to see at least one in a particular position. He seemed to read my mind and extended a forepaw exactly as I wanted to see it. Then he put that paw in my hand. I had no camera so made a mental picture and later carved the pipe the way he showed me.

~~~~~~~~~~~~~~~~~~~

Indigenous people in the Americas have good reasons to revere Jaguar and Puma. Essentially, Jaguar and Puma are consummate purveyors of ayni. In earlier times when there was more sharing between man and animal, these cats took a lot from the people, including their lives. In exchange, Jaguar and Puma provide tremendous knowledge, gifts of power and accompaniment into the lower realms, revealing and thereby shapeshifting our subconscious fears. Often invisible even in full sunlight, Jaguar and Puma are superb hunters in and of the night, em-
~~~~~~~~~~~~~~~~~~~

bodying stealth, speed, power, grace, courage and cunning. The spotted fur of Jaguar represents the stars of the Milky Way, and Puma, the sun. Jaguar and Puma are integral and ancestral recipients of ayni. When they are eliminated, ayni must be given in other ways.

The following story, then, is not meant to be insensitive, especially if you keep in mind Jaguar's and Puma's traditional relationship with us through ayni. The story is simply a possible expanded view of possibility.

Lost Youth

I didn't know where I was going when I left the house that day. After meandering through the hills, I drove to a trailhead in the Absaroka Mountains, started up the trail, then up switchbacks to the top of a waterfall. I got there late in the afternoon as the sun was setting behind orange and mauve colored clouds. A high school student fell from there a few years before and was killed. Extremely athletic and a competitive gymnast, he was known for his wit, charm and vibrant energy. A bit off the trail there is a rock cairn and an angel statue near the site dedicated to his memory. I was drawn there to pray.

The scenery was spectacular. Pine Creek churned to my right, before it tumbled over the cliff and flowed with the south fork. I could not see the bottom of the canyon, but as I looked toward the sunset I saw the Paradise Valley where the Yellowstone River flows and beyond that, more mountains to the west.

Some of the rocks in the cairn were huge and all were really rounded. It seemed they came from the creek, but when I looked around for a rounded rock to add to the cairn, I could not find one. I looked in the creek and around the area, but all the rocks were jagged. It's possible the young man's friends brought these rocks up from below. I was reluctant to get into the water and root around for a rock in case I slipped over the falls. I can be kind of clumsy. In any case, I did not find anything that felt right. I resigned myself to what I could easily get, so reached down and separated a piece of rock from rock and soil, cleaned it and took it to the cairn. I tried to fit it in a couple of places, but nothing quite worked until I found a place at the top of the cairn where the stone literally clicked into place in a small opening between two rocks, like the top piece of an apacheta, a ceremonially-built rock cairn. I realized then it looked like the right hand of a mitten, with the thumb out in a shamanic salute. I saluted back.

Then it came to me that maybe this teen's life and body were accepted as an offering by the mountains and the waterfall, not as a conscious act on the part of the young man, but as a way to imbue that place with his energy and life. It was as if his spirit might have been waiting for someone to acknowledge that and to appreciate what happened there. So I did and prayed for his peace, the peace of his family and thanked him. The angel statue has a small solar cell connected to it so it glows at night. It's really a beautiful spot. I felt the spirit was grateful. I lingered a while, then started back down the trail.

I am amazed at how many good and beautiful young people are lost in such ways. We all know of them. I do not know if they are taken from us or if they give themselves for us, as they are the best we have, or if inexplicable accidents just happen. People have died for causes for centuries; maybe ayni is one of them. Few jaguar and puma are around to extract and accept ayni these days. Rivers, lakes, mountains and oceans may receive the offerings instead. Hence it is important for all of us to engage in sacred reciprocity so the obligation is carried by many rather than a few.

~~~~~~~~~~~~~~~~~~~
~~~~~~~~~~~~~~~~~~~

5

Worrier to Warrior

"Everything comes from the light; even the dark."
don Oscar Miro-Quesada

In the African country of Cameroon, the Mofu people survive a harsh life by planting millet, their main food crop. The success of the crop depends upon timely rains and the people's tribute to their ancestors. Without either, their seeds and crops may be devoured by black ants and termites, which can have a better life than the people, since they usually find something to eat.

One year, the rains were late. As a group of elders talked about the problem with their chief, one man added that termites were throughout his home's walls and getting close to his granary. Nothing he had done stopped them and part of his roof caved in. He asked for help.

It was decided to call in the Jaglavak, a specific type of army ant that kills termites, but can also attack people and livestock. The villagers knew that to invite the Jaglavak could cause worse problems than the termites, but if the termites spread to other houses and granaries the people would be wiped out.

All of this is captured in a NOVA documentary titled *Master of the Killer Ants.* It is must watching for anyone interested in the importance of giving sacred reciprocity and creating sacred space, as well as a primer on how to make effective prayer. Human survival is at stake, and nothing focuses intent as when we have our backs against the wall, especially when that wall is collapsing from termites and we stand to lose everything. Reading some of the disparaging viewer comments on this video, however, shows many people aren't willing to even consider alternative possibilities to how things can work. It seems these viewers have not experienced any reality other than the one described to and prescribed for them. Nor do they know anything about quantum physics.

The documentary stresses the importance of many relationships, with gratitude among the most important. We can probably agree that to say thank you for something given to us is good manners. And there are many ways to sincerely say thank you through words, gestures and deeds. However, requiring others to thank you can become controlling, such as holding up a cookie to a child and making him say "Thank you" before he gets it. We may have learned early that receiving is conditional rather than reciprocal. That makes all the difference in the world. Instead of a flow of giving and receiving, potential abundance becomes a dribble of behaving in order to have. It is well known among child development professionals that children sense their dependence on the adults charged with caring for them, and behave accordingly. Once bright-eyed, unlimited beings learn to behave to have, they can become puppets rather than thoughtful and sensitive participants. Adults who role model interdependence, rather than dependence or greed, contribute to everyone's abundance. Abundance is more flowing when the conditions are based on appropriate expression rather than solely on behavior. The Inca, for example, had and have a simple formula for appropriate behavior and civil expression: Don't lie. Don't steal. Don't be lazy. As long as those three conditions are met, a person's freedom and communal sustenance are assured.

Appropriate behavior is important, but ayni is a better social skill than disconnected behavior modification imposed upon a child, when neither the child nor the adult really knows what's going on. Such conditioning squanders our health and our natural and spiritual resources. It can mold us into ungrateful, ungraceful people because we aren't happy. Many studies show how important making positive contributions are to our positive social development. Ayni encourages children to become sincerely grateful, responsible and connected rather than controlled, spoiled or entitled. The biggest reason may be because the child is involved in something meaningful and knows his or her actions make a difference. Kids who see and participate in ayni get a feeling of belonging. It can put them in touch with lifelong curiosity steeped in imagination and right action, and giving and receiving. Ayni will do wonders for a child's sensitivity, intuition, compassion and connection. And remember, the planet reciprocates with magic! That will light up their little hearts.

The onslaught of negative peer pressure can be another source for giving away one's power. It can also leave parents absolutely bewildered by their child's behavior. In her book *Developing Your Backbone: the science of saying NO*, Anne Brown, PhD writes, "Researchers have found we are more effective in our interpersonal interactions when we are more open and aware of our blindnesses. The more authentically we speak, the more successful we will be in our career, our love life, our family, and with our health and our friends. If our speaking and actions are driven by honesty, we will be in the world with authenticity, power, passion, dignity, peace and success." However, a child connected to the planet can be the more influential peer and demonstrate to his or her friends ways to positively empower themselves. Ayni can do this through developing a greater connection. That greater connection simply puts more imagination and information and creative energy into the hands and heart of the child, thus building the authenticity needed for healthy living. Generosity and reciprocity support authenticity, but don't make up for a lack of it.

Sacred reciprocity teaches and shows that we are not special because we are special. We are special because we are equal. Hence, feelings of entitlement or being a puppet give way to equanimity. When life pushes us to our limits and beyond, ayni can provide the bulwark against being absolutely crushed.

During the darkest nights of the soul, however, when we are brutalized, bludgeoned by losses and abandoned, giving sacred thanks can seem like a joke. It is almost impossible to muster sincere gratitude when we are angry with the Creator and life. Once we realize nothing we do in life will ever buffer us completely from the pains of life and what the soul needs, we can embrace ayni and the dark night at the crossroads of surrender to the truth of our soul. This helps dismember our longing for what Caroline Myss calls a search for "a logical and reasonable god," and reinforces that life is larger than our particular struggles.

The term Dark Night of the Soul came from the title of a poem written by St. John of the Cross around 1578, while John was imprisoned for trying to reform his Carmelite order. Although the term initially centered on a spiritual crisis, it has become more encompassing. Today the dark night is a euphemism for "The shit has hit the fan...and I can't come up for air." It will likely last months if not years, although in Aaron Ralston's case it lasted hours and for Mother Teresa, nearly a lifetime. The soul may sense it coming and think it is ready for it. Or, something may hit out of the blue, so to speak: the death of a loved one or a relationship, and/or a physical, mental, emotional or spiritual trauma. One loss can trigger a series of losses, pile driving the soul ever deeper beyond depression into the depths of hopelessness, shattered faith and, well, darkness. During the dark night it seems impossible to garner the slightest uplift from the vibration of the memory of good times, as good memories may be one of the triggers of real funk. The dark night is a crisis in consciousness, of belief, a psycho-physio shattering and dismembering of energy, leading to what some call chaos.

When a person, especially in western culture, begins to understand the importance of ayni, that is, true sacred reciprocity as an integral part of life, it can signify the person is on the verge of a split with something old, or on the verge of connecting with something new. Ayni can put the soul on the threshold of the dark night or it can be the lifeline as one plummets towards the depths of the dark night. A sincere appreciation for something one has or the perfect clarity that something needs to go, such as when Aaron Ralston cut off his arm to release himself from being pinned by a boulder for 127 hours in a slot canyon, can make one grateful for the experience.

Ayni won't keep the dark night away. "What doesn't kill us makes us stronger," is not nearly as true as "What doesn't make us stronger, kills us," especially if it is a slow and painful death by a thousand cuts to the heart. During the dark night, we'd almost give anything to have things back the way they were, but going back is not an option when falling. Nothing can stop the soul's inevitable surrender to releasing what must go. It is simply a question of when, not if. Ayni helps the soul find and live with soul, but it cannot stop the Dark Night of the Soul.

In a reality of unconditional and unlimited love, the Dark Night of the Soul is not punishment, although it seems that way. We can mask it, deny it, subvert it, pervert it, but we can never destroy it. The dark night is a calling. We can make choices that put us out of love's way, but, ultimately, love is the path of our own heart. As much as anything, this is what ayni returns to us. This is the magic; this is the paradox: the heart must be broken for it to open. So, we cannot live from the heart until we heal the heart. In other words, it takes heart to live with heart. Of course, ayni may never figure into a Dark Night at all, but if it does, the spirits who have come to know you through your offerings will hold your heart and make the suffering at least a little more bearable, even when you are pissed at the world and the gods or the Creator. An angel even comforted Jesus during the dark night before his crucifixion, but he still had to go through it.

Ayni invites an altered state because it connects us with something other than the self. Ayni gets us out of ourselves, much as does a dream. It blends and bends reality into a dream landscape of natural signs, talking streams and animate rocks. Whenever we are present, or mindful, and simply close our eyes, our brain immediately produces more alpha waves, the bridge state between theta, a meditative or light dreaming state, and beta, the conscious, rationale mind. So ayni creates a waking dream state of imagination, surrealism and receptivity to the denizens of nature as they basically say, "That two-legged over there is giving thanks on our turf on our terms. Let's have a closer look-see." In western science, a bell rings and a dog salivates. In shamanic science a bell rings and spirits come in to see what you want. Sometimes they salivate, too.

Life is hard enough as is without us working to intentionally make it harder on anyone living with us or after us. Indigenous wisdom – also known as common sense – encourages us to make decisions on behalf of the next seven generations, so they may enjoy what we have today, or something a little better. Of course there is never total agreement on what better is, but there could likely be some points of agreement, such as clean and abundant air and water for future generations. Those two energies alone would assure a natural and naturally vibrant planet with diverse life. That seems like a good place to start. That means we'll have something pretty good, too. Each generation owes it to future generations to clean up its messes so future generations are free to make their own mistakes without having to step into the crap of the ones who came before them. For the most part, we hold kindergarteners to higher standards than we do our leaders and ourselves, especially when it comes to sharing, being kind, taking responsibility and cleaning messes. Our legacy should be their foundation, not their frontier.

It may be difficult, if not impossible, to earn a heavenly paradise or to consciously evolve, if we do not take care of this earthly one. We may need to show we can take care of this one before we can move on. To leave the planet a little better than how we found it is not an onerous dictum. Even if it is difficult to imagine and come to a consensus on what that is, inherently we all know what it isn't. The concept of considering seven generations is a futuristic and healthy bond with the past. Keeping the slate clean does not mean there is no connection with the past. If anything, it enhances a connection. It offers an unencumbered view and appreciation of what past generations have done. As Edmund Burke wrote, "Those who do not know history are doomed to repeat it." Understanding history leads to change, not stagnation.

Legacy of the Flying D

I used to live outside of Gallatin Gateway, Montana along the beautiful Gallatin River. Shortly after I moved there, media mogul Ted Turner bought the Flying D Ranch, historically managed as a cattle ranch. You may have heard of Ted. You may have even heard Ted, as he was once known as The Mouth of the South. Once married to Jane Fonda, he now has several girl friends, claiming that that can be complicated, but not as complicated as being married.

Ted doesn't like cattle. He met with all the Flying D cowboys and told them that. He also told them each one of them would have a job as long as they did things his way, which is common when someone works for someone, and that he was going to run bison, not cattle. A lot of Montana cowboys couldn't handle that, so quit. Many could, so they stayed. In any case, Ted had his workers tear out all the interior barbed wire fences, as bison walk right through them, and install stout, high-voltage electric fences and gates to control the animals' movement from one river drainage to the next. The Flying D covers 113,613-acres, and goes from the Gallatin River to the Madison River and beyond. Bison are a moneymaker for him. They provide meat to Ted's restaurants and the ranch is also managed for wildlife production for guided hunting. So, Ted is a good capitalist and environmentalist, has had a tremendous and positive impact on amateur and professional sports, and is a proponent of free speech and hard work. Once at a Bozeman-area Chamber of Commerce meeting at which Turner was a guest speaker to a hostile crowd he said, "A lot of people don't like that fact I own the Flying D. To them I say, 'If you don't like what I'm doing, get your own three billion dollars and you can do whatever you want, too.'" That's what he was "worth" then.

Mountain streams from the Flying D flow into the Gallatin and Madison rivers, providing great spawning areas for native cutthroat trout, a threatened species. The mountains and grasslands on the "D" provide habitat and forage for all sorts of native wildlife. Wildlife and native plants from the D disperse to the rest of the area, helping seed new populations. As the second largest private land owner in the country, his landholdings help preserve the environmental integrity that supports tourism, hunting, fishing, agriculture and even environmental organizations.

Why do people dislike him? Because he does and gets what he wants, which is really what all of us want to do, but don't know how? And a lot of what Ted does is gives back...back to the planet and the preservation of the planet for future generations. Much of his land, a total of 2 million acres in all of his combined properties, is in conservation easements. And most of his money will go to charity when he passes. So what's the problem? Why do we treat such people with disdain? Why do we belittle and devalue what gives back. Why? If this is the prevailing pervasive attitude toward ayni and looking ahead to the traditional seven generations, what does this say about our culture and us?

I say a little thank you to and for Ted every time I drive on his access road to get into the backcountry, which I'll do even after I get my own three billion dollars.

~~~~~~~~~~~~~~~~~~~

Virtually every known culture throughout human history gave back to the planet in a ceremonial way for her life sustaining abundance. Many still do. In this time of rapid planetary change, sacred reciprocity is a way to gain a measure of control and direction over life without being controlled or directed. Does the planet ask us to say thank you? Not really. She doesn't hold cookies in front of our little
~~~~~~~~~~~~~~~~~~~

faces and tell us to beg. Like the loving mother she is, she'll give to us until she has nothing left. And she does. This is her way. Ceremony tunes us with the rhythm of the planet. Truly thanking a tree or a butterfly or a robin or a worm simply for being begins to unravel the fabricated veil between the natural world and us, between the magical world and us.

This veil is astonishingly thin. It seems to take a 24/7 onslaught from a world of distraction to distract us from that which gives us life and makes life worth living. Any action away from this distraction weakens the veil and strengthens our ability to reach across the veil. It enlarges our reality and hence our understanding of what is or what may be. Any act of sacred reciprocity puts a magical momentum of awareness in place as we come to realize that everything with which we share this planet has been aware of us all along. When life no longer runs from us for its own survival, we take one another in a mutual embrace of transformation. Sometimes this takes place at feeding time, and everything eats, one way or the other. We quit reciprocating when we forget there's enough to go around to give back to what sustains us. In an unlimited, abundant universe, there is more than enough for every one and that is the kind of universe in which we live. Giving and receiving are the essence of magic, introducing us to the processes of shapeshifting, of being and becoming and continual renewal. This is how we learn to be grateful without being controlled. This is how we learn to have without having to behave because we are mindful of whom and what comes after us. By offering ayni, we sanctify ourselves and the space in which we give.

We all know life is hard on just about everything that lives. It's certainly tough on us, but the majority of us get enough air to breathe, water to drink and food to eat. We get around. We get love. We laugh. The flow that brings us a little is the same process that can bring us a lot. We should discern what lack is caused by natural cycles and what is caused by our choices; understanding the difference impacts our actions. Sacred reciprocity is a spigot that opens the flow. It can support our physical sustenance so we are free to embark upon soul nourishing physical, mental, emotional and spiritual adventures. These reduce the amount of physical resources we need as we become more balanced and have more access to very subtle, but very real, alternatives to the material world. Consequently, pulling more subtle resources into our physical environment and activities is one way we participate in the transformation of light to fire to light, that is from spirit to matter to spirit. And what is spirit? I like to use Jack Schwarz's definition: spirit is pure, undiluted, unadulterated energy. People who are in the flow don't fear other people who are in the flow and sure don't try to stop others from getting into it. All these work together to help us become more human. Ayni strengthens our connection and consciousness. Ayni is not a Get out of Jail Free card, one that allows us to be stupid when we are not reciprocating, but it is key to mutually assured survival.

There can be no response without consciousness. Plants and animals respond favorably to us; some research suggests that water does, too. Extending our relationships from pets and houseplants to the natural world will build even stronger ties among us. Yet, with the evidence all around us, we are encouraged to live in denial of the possible and of what we are capable. The planet is either magical or it is not. So we either engage with it or we do not. If the planet isn't magical, then neither is life and that seems unlikely. If magic doesn't exist, why don't we create it the way we create so much other stuff? If it does exist, why don't we use it? Either way, we are ignoring the opportunities magic offers.

I confess. I believe in magic. Magic directs us to take right action without thinking about it first. Magic serves us as we serve ayni. Whereas technology attempts to give us control over our environment – it really doesn't - magic connects us with it. That is the definitive difference between the two. As a matter of fact, there is growing concern about just how much technology, specifically the field of Artificial Intelligence, is controlling our behavior rather than us controlling its behavior. Ayni may reduce this possibility by helping us develop human potentials and a behavior foreign to AI – at least for now. Is modern technology the anti-magic? I don't think so. It simply needs to be questioned in terms of its impacts on the planet and us and adapted to us, rather than requiring us to adapt to it.

6

Creating Sacred Space

"[Sacred space] is an absolute necessity for anybody today... It's the place of creative incubation. At first you may find that nothing happens there. But if you have a sacred place and use it, something eventually will happen."
Joseph Campbell

What is sacred space? Let's look at it in three basic ways: personal, public and inner. Personal sacred space is created in a home or private area. It usually consists of a personal prayer, meditation or ceremonial area, indoors or out. Public sacred space is a public ceremonial site – a sacred structure, shrine, cemetery or any area maintained for public praying and honoring – or a natural sacred site, such as a grove of trees, a mountain or a rock outcropping. The inner sacred is the state of a person's head and heart at any time or space. Naturally, this extends beyond the physical boundary of a person's body. Inner and outer sacred space influence one another.

Sacred space and sacred reciprocity go hand in hand. Every act of reciprocity strengthens our connection to the magical, reciprocal world. Ayni consistently given in the same sacred space tends to strengthen the connection even more. Such a space becomes like a spiritual watering hole, desirable for both giver and receiver. Sacred space is made more sacred by the consistent intent and actions there, as the area tends to hold the vibrations of prayer and reciprocity. Any area in which we pay reverent homage changes to a higher vibration, which is one reason why public sacred places begin to feel, well, sacred! More on vibration later, as that term gets tossed around a lot without much explanation.

Think of sacred space as a spiritual workshop, a place with character suitable to its proposed purpose. Most sacred space contains sacred items. These are usually items a person has made, received or bought from another, from nature or the spirit world. The intent and power of those items varies. Some items provide comfort and protection. Some may be used for healing. Others aid illumination, divination or shape-shifting. Still others help focus a person's intent.

Space is full of energy. Sacred spaces develop a unique energetic feel. By way of comparison, a butcher shop will feel much different than a bakery, although both provide food. A bookstore may feel comparable to a library, but the operation of each serves different needs. A cathedral might beckon prayerful intent, wilderness may release intent and both could leave a person feeling humble.

Maintaining a sacred reciprocal connection through maintaining sacred space is a responsibility in many cultures. It's not an option. It's not superstition. It is the hallmark of an advanced and conscious people. There are many sacred sites throughout the world. Some remain in much their natural state, such as Devil's Tower in Wyoming, traditionally known as Mato Tipila, or Bear's Lodge, to the Lakota people. Others, such as France's Chartres Cathedral, are emblematic of sacred public sites.

Throughout antiquity and into modern times, monument building has often been a way to combine prayer and reciprocity, especially temple and ceremonial sites. These include Mesoamerican pyramids, prayer wheels, cathedrals, mosques, stone shrines, and obelisks on such sacred sites. Human activity and intention can bring and maintain sacredness to just about any place or accentuate the natural. No matter how well known or unknown sites are, it can be safely said that every tribe and most families have at least one place sacred to it.

Let's focus on personal sacred space and inner sacred space. We won't be concerned with public sacred space. We can tie into the grid of sacred and earth-based energies, honoring and amplifying sacred space through ceremony. This raises the vibration of both the ritualist and the area, and connects them almost in ways lovers are connected.

That may sound absurd to someone who does not have a connection with a sacred space, but it is true. Raising and sharing vibration is one of the best gifts we can give anything or anyone. Think of sacred space as the stage or arena from which seen and unseen audiences receive offerings. It's common for members of this audience to become performers on stage, as well.

When within our personal sacred space, the first space to consider is the head-heart connection. This doesn't imply the rest of the body isn't important, but this is a great place to start and it starts with breathing.

Few things connect us physically to ourself, each other and keep us in the moment as does breathing. How we breathe and how much oxygen we have in our blood and body give all sorts of signals to our mental-emotional state. Not only does how we breathe impact our mental-emotional state, but our mental-emotional state impacts how we breathe. Presence is present in breathing. Breathing oxygen that has been part of life for eons connects us with the cycles of life and creation, bridging us within the timelessness of everything that has gone before and exists now to give us what we have. Drinking a glass of water can do the same thing, as water has been in cycle on our planet for billions of years, longer than oxygen. That multi-billion-year-old water is the same water we drink today. As a matter of fact, the water on earth is older than our sun.

Why is air sacred? Some creation stories explain that air is the breath of the Creator and so through breathing, the Creator gives us life. Imagining that the air we breathe is the breath of the Creator should assure that when we speak it will be done respectfully to the sacred world and to everything we encounter. And to breathe the same air used by all great teachers to oxygenate our brains to come up with thoughts that are then spoken vilely towards another is not its highest use. If we need to count to ten before speaking, that's what we should do, but if we remember that this very same air was, or will be, used by someone we love that may not be necessary.

We have a choice: whether or not to use our breath for the highest good. Imagine revering the air by never using it to say anything demeaning or stupid. Think what that alone would do to change the planet. How much climate change occurs because we get into heated arguments? What we think and say should not pollute the air we breathe. Breathe consciously; speak respectfully.

Air is also extraordinary. The balance of the atmosphere is such that the relatively heavy concentration of nitrogen in it, required for protein synthesis, dilutes the oxygen enough to prevent rapid burning on the surface of the earth. The narrow range of conditions in which life as we know it endures, and everything the planet does to maintain this balance, is truly magical. We are enveloped in the miraculous, by the marvelous. We really should be awed at least once a day.

There are many breathing patterns and visualizations appropriate for meditation and ayni. So, I will offer only general guidelines and rhythms here that should complement any breathing practice. I encourage you to try this a few times, and then adapt it to what works better for you.

Unlike a glass that fills from the bottom up, the lungs fill from the top down. So, deep breathing is active – not strenuous – but active in order to fill the lungs close to capacity by pulling air down into the lungs. Without breathing deeply, we accumulate a pool of stagnant air at the base of our lungs, which I refer to as a reverse bio-inversion layer, trapped by incoming air. Here's how to get it out.

First, breathe in through the nose by gently pushing the abdomen out. Known as abdominal breathing, this fills the top half of the lungs or so, and relaxes the body. Shallow breathing, which is also called clavicular breathing, can happen when we get scared or surprised and tells the body to get ready to take action. The air tends to stay in the upper lungs with clavicular breathing. Whereas it may not matter if the glass is half empty or half full, it makes a major difference with the lungs.

Practice abdominal breathing for a few breaths. Then, go into true deep breathing. This is done by powerfully pulling the abdomen *in* on the inhalation. This allows the diaphragm – which separates the heart and lungs from the abdominal cavity - to contract and move down as much as possible, moving out of the way of the lungs so they can fill more fully. A powerful inhalation allows for a long exhalation, which helps achieve what some call mind-body harmony, a relaxed state of mind and body. Giving the body plenty of oxygen tells it it is not under stress. This is why shallow breathing can be so counterproductive; it accentuates unease, which may lead to disease. When I want to maximize my air intake, I take a powerful inhalation by pulling the abdomen in to get the diaphragm out of the way, although as the lower lungs fill, the abdomen goes back out. When I cannot take any more air in that way, I continue to inhale as I raise my shoulders toward my ears. This fills the top of the lungs to complete the breath. By the way, I breathe pulling the abdomen in all the time, not just when I get ready to get right. I consciously pull the abdomen in and visualize oxygen-energy coursing all the way to the base of my spine throughout the day. This improves posture, which helps maximize lung capacity. Some even say it mitigates back pain.

If you already breathe by pulling the abdomen in, don't change by forcing it out. However, if you need to practice deep breathing, lie on your back with a pillow under your knees. Inhale through the nose and allow the abdomen to rise. Put a hand on your abdomen and one on your chest. The hand on your abdomen should go up; the hand on your chest should rise little, if at all, and then only at the end of your inhalation. When happy with that after a few breaths, breathe in through the nose and draw the abdomen in as you inhale. Increase the speed and power of your inhalations to pull air deeply into your lungs. Exhale slowly.

Now sit up straight and relax. Sit in a chair or wherever you want to be comfortable. Breathing patterns and visualizations can help regulate our energy. They can energize us for when we need to deal with something in front of us or slow us down to get us into the mind-body state appropriate for non-ordinary reality. For now, breathe in and out of the nose. An easy and relaxing breathing pattern is the following:

Inhale for a count of 8
Hold for a count of 4
Exhale for a count of 8
Hold out for a count of 4

When ready, inhale by powerfully pulling the abdomen in as the count changes to

Inhale for 4
Hold for 4
Exhale for 16

Hold out for 4

Then…

Inhale for 4
Hold for 4
Exhale for 24
Hold out for 4
Then…

Inhale for 4
Hold for 4
Exhale for 32
Hold out for 4

A powerful and complete inhalation into the lower lungs makes the long exhalation possible. Raise your shoulders toward your ears at the end of your inhalation, if you want, to fill the very top of your lungs. Try to go to a 48 then a 64 count exhalation. Keep the tongue, jaws, head, face and neck relaxed. Adding visualization can intensify the experience. But first, take your left palm and find the hottest part of your head. (The left hand is more sensitive to heat. I am blessed with not having a lot of hair, so I can do this easily.) Most people will find the hottest part of the head is the crown and it can really heat up during some of these breathing techniques. That's an indication of more energy coming in through your head. Isn't it interesting that we may have never noticed this before, and yet we've had our crown with us our whole life?

Now pull energy through your crown as you inhale. Imagine your crown chakra opening up like a flower and pure and powerful light energy – white or gold usually – coming through your head and down your spine. Allow it to pool at the base of your spine and lower abdomen. Hold that breath and energy for a count of four and then exhale out your hands, feet and forehead. Pour it out as you exhale, like water shooting out of a fire hose. Amp it up. Do this several times.

Next, begin to breathe to activate your heart space. As you inhale, pull energy into your heart from your chest and from the first thoracic vertebrae of your spine, which is slightly above your physical heart.

This is considered to be the anchor point of the heart chakra. This way energy comes in from two directions, from your chest and spine. Hold in, allowing the energy to fill your heart and entire chest cavity. Then exhale out your heart, through your chest, into the space around you.

Allow these visualizations to change. Start off with them or with whatever your body and intuition reveal to you, but allow the energy to change how you take it in, hold it and let it go. The energy will normally stay at a bright level, but if it darkens, just keep at it until it's transformed to a higher vibration. A darkening of energy simply means you are releasing toxin or stagnation.

When ready, let the visualization and breathing pattern go, and allow your body to establish its own breathing rhythm. The intent is to be at peace in mind and body, but also energized and alert and to fill your sacred space with the powerful, connected, compassionate and grateful energy of your heart. I think of this as heart breathing.

Sometimes I chum the cosmos, that is I create a feeling and visualization in tune with my intent, which is one of appreciation and joy when I offer ayni. In time, this feeling becomes authentic, so yes, I may imagine it if I'm not at my best, and I will use breathing as a detox. In other words, creating the feeling to emulate intent is another option to try. Some people say, "Fake it 'til you make it." I don't want to go quite that far. I choose to be more in a process of transformation than denial and acknowledge how I am. I've found that simply intending to be at a high level of connection and peace when I sit in sacred space overcomes a down mood. That is a purpose of ceremony, to get into right relationship, to shapeshift into a higher way of being, without ignoring how I feel. And, the space in which I normally do this, as well as the sacred objects and allies I have also help. It almost always turns into a happy time for all of us. A walk, some exercise or stretching beforehand helps, too.

So, to prepare for sacred reciprocity, breathe deeply, exhale generously. If we are mindful of the cycles we embody and in which we engage, we can more easily use energy-oxygen for the highest and greatest good. If we imagine that's what others do, too, our appreciation toward them will grow. Begin to create sacred space by consciously inhaling the sacred vitality of air. Allow the oxygen to sanctify body and thoughts, generating a feeling of infinite peace, nourishment and eternal connection. Exhale vibrantly into the sacred space, allowing the vibration of mind and body to vivify the space and fill it all around you. In this way, become a co-creator of that sacred space. Connect with it.

When the head is clear and calm, sanctify the heart with the breathing. Intend the oxygen-energy to engage the heart. Frequently people visualize the heart or heart chakra in meditation, which is great, but they are not the same thing. Nor is there universal acceptance on what the heart chakra is. As the heart is often considered to be the seat of consciousness and gold is often referred to as the color of consciousness, it seems unlikely that green is the color of the heart chakra, which some suggest. Other teachers, including Jack Schwarz, say the heart chakra is gold.[2] That is what my experience tells me. The thing is, we are not trying to maintain our chakras at a specific color or energy level. The goal is to vibrate at the highest level possible, which is normally considered to be a radiant white. For now it will suffice to energize the heart space with breathing and feeling.

Researches have measured that the heart gives out a lot more electrical current than the brain does. Not only that, but the heart sends more information to the brain than visa versa[3]. Some of the best scientific and practical information of how this works is available through the Heartmath Institute. Science also suggests that some of a person's memory may be stored in the heart. But forget about science for a moment and key on experience. If you have ever been in love or had your heart "broken," you are well aware that the heart feels. It seems when we get love, our capacity to give love increases. Sending this love into sacred space energizes it and raises its vibration. Quantum physics supports this. We are energy. We are surrounded by energy. Our intent impacts energy, which impacts manifestation. But if you encounter a skeptic, simply remind them that reason good research requires double blind and triple blind studies is to keep the researchers' intent from in-

---

[2] For a complete discussion of one chakra system, I recommend Jack's book, *Voluntary Controls*, a meditation classic.

[3] Traditionally scientists believed it was the brain that sent information and issued commands to the body, including the heart, but physiology studies now claim the reverse is true as well. "Research has shown that the heart communicates to the brain in four major ways: neurologically (through the transmission of nerve impulses), biochemically (via hormones and neurotransmitters), biophysically (through pressure waves) and energetically (through electromagnetic field interactions)," Heartmath Institute researchers explain in Science of the Heart, an overview of research conducted by the institute.

fluencing results. You can follow up with, "If intent influences results, but is kept out of the results, then where do the results come from?" If followed through far enough, we may come to the conclusion that belief is behind any result, that is, belief determines what we interpret to be true. Physical reality is based on belief, which is generated from imagination. More on that later.

Back to the heart. The heart is our feeling center. Feeling generates more energy than thought, documented by the scientifically measured energetic level of the heart. When thought and feeling are in harmony, we don't send mixed messages. We send focused intent. Space becomes sacred through the focused intent of head and heart *in right relationship*, thereby creating a space that receives and responds to sacred reciprocity. The heart chakra emits its incredible energy also due to the fact of its role of energetic transmutation. It receives subtle energies from the higher chakra centers and alters their vibration for physical use. It also channels energy from the lower centers, preparing them for more subtle expression. This is what is meant by transmuting subtle human energies from light to fire to light. The heart chakra is the holy grail of this process.

I almost always smudge my space and myself before I start a ceremony. Sometimes I do this before and sometimes after I get my head and heart right through breathing and mental focus. Smudging is simply infusing space and blessing yourself with incense, aromatic plants and/or oils. Such fragrances make us feel good and clear the air. Spirits like them, too.

If you already follow a tradition, then there are smudge items you likely use in specific ways. If not, study a tradition that attracts you and go with that, or find out what traditional cultures are or were alive and well where you live now and consider using their ways. Recent studies show that smudging is anti-bacterial and will keep a room clear of a long list of bacteria hours after smudging. Smudging is often done with a feather or a fan of some sort.

The following is information about four plants commonly used by some North American tribes for smudges and offerings: sage, sweetgrass, cedar and tobacco.

Sage – There are several types of sage. Every summer I pick my annual supply of sage, the herbaceous prairie sage, not sagebrush. It grows wild in Montana. I don't take too much from any one area. I was taught to pull it up by the roots so the spirit of the plant comes with it. Of course, I smudge myself before I collect, and then leave periodic offerings of tobacco and maybe other things to some of the larger "chief" plants I encounter, which I never take. I ask each plant to come with me before I pull it. If I have to exert more than a moderate pull to take the plant, I leave it. Most plants come quite easily. Those that don't, I don't take. I dry and store the plants in a dark, cool area. Sagebrush leaves may also be used. If you collect sagebrush, cut the branches with pruners, then strip the leaves from the branches. Remember to leave offerings.

Sage smudge clears, cleans and protects. I use a lot of it in ceremony. When smudging inside, it's a great idea to have at least one window open, even in winter, so the bad *jhu-jhu* the smudge activates can leave the space. I don't burn the stalks when I smudge just for myself inside or outside. I strip the leaves and roll them in a loose ball and burn the leaves in an abalone shell – which represents water – or other fireproof container. I rub the smoke over my hands and the rest of my body. Once when my girl friend's feet were cold, I smudged her feet and they stayed warm the rest of the afternoon on a hike. I keep the stalks and when there is a sacred fire, such as for a sweat, I toss them in it with my appreciation.

Sweetgrass is another traditional herb. It smells good, so it is used to purify thoughts, which helps clear the space. When buying sweetgrass, one usually finds sweetgrass in braids. To use it, light the tip and waft it around to let the smoke fill the space. A braid can last a long time. It grows wild in various parts of Canada and the U.S., and more people are growing it in the yard or garden. It's a perennial and can be harvested annually. The roots are not taken. Cut it with a knife or scissors three or four inches above ground level. When you get a bunch of it and want to make a braid, one way is to tie off the cut end of the bunch with sweetgrass or thread and separate it into three strands. Hold the strands between the balls of your feet and start braiding. Tie off the top end and dry it outside.

Incense cedar or **flat cedar** is often mixed with sage for smudge. Cedar preserves, which is why it's used in cedar chests. Cedar preserves good intentions and good space. I get mine from friends, and when I travel to areas where it grows in the mountains. It's easy to find in stores and online, though.

Tobacco – Domestic tobacco is not used as a smudge that I know of. There are many variations of this plant, wild and domestic. When I load my *cannupa*[4], which is a Lakota word loosely translated as two wood and refers to the pipe bowl and stem of the sacred pipe, I use a smoking mixture I make, not store bought tobacco, but tobacco is a generic term that can mean smoking mixture. However, store tobacco is frequently left as an offering. For offerings I use the Native American Spirit brand, organic variety, when I can find it. Some of my friends will roll a smoke when they are at a sweat lodge fire and smoke it to begin the ceremony. Others toss hand rolled or store bought cigarettes or loose leaf tobacco into the fire as an offering. Tobacco is used because it absorbs prayers and intentions. So, a pinch of tobacco is held and the prayer is put into it. A separate pinch is often offered to each of the seven directions, which are the four cardinal directions, the sky, the earth and the heart. As an aside, smoking a mixture in a *cannupa* releases those seven direction prayers. The smoke is not inhaled. Smoking the *cannupa* can be thought of as sending prayerful intent across the veil and into the higher dimensions of Spirit.

Following this or a similar process, the four basic elements of water, earth, fire and air are represented in the sacred space. The abalone or seashell represents water. The plant materials represent earth. Burning the smudge represents fire. Fanning the smudge with a feather or fan represents air. The fifth element of sacred space is the space, which is not empty, but full of energy. It has many other names including etheric energy, akasha, sami, the vivifying force, chi, ki and prana.

Other items to use for personal smudge or space clearing can be things such as copal or frankincense, which are tree resins, palo santo, a fragrant wood, essential oils, and whatever is part of a tradition to which you are drawn. Lavender is also a favorite. I keep some in a glass by my altar and stir it up from time to time, like a potpourri. Throughout Mesoamerica, copal resin is considered a gift from the "god of lightning," who passed his power on to a copal tree, after it was struck by lightning. Burn resins and woods in a sturdy fireproof container. I have a miniature cast iron skillet ashtray that works great, especially

---

[4] The bowl represents the feminine; the stem represents the masculine. When bowl and stem join, the pipe represents universal and primal creative powers, and connects prayerful intent with those powers.

when I burn incense charcoal in it for the resins. But always put the container on a potholder or something similar, as it can get hot, especially when burning charcoal. Lit candles in your space are also a nice touch. I use unscented beeswax candles.[5]

Naturally, the state of the heart and mind – the inner space – is the most important sacred space. Yet, as everything is connected, I am reluctant to write that. But if I am distracted or my mood isn't right, smudging and sitting with my altar can alter my inner space for the better. Willing the mind and heart to be at peace may take practice, so here are some tips.

After smudging, sit comfortably within your outer sacred space. I sit cross-legged in front of my altar or where I meditate. It's fine to sit on a chair, in which some people sit cross-legged, some cross just their ankles and others put their feet flat on the floor. Some meditation teachers suggest sitting cross-legged when you are alone to contain energy, but to sit with legs uncrossed when you are with others to allow for an exchange of energy. For a freer flow of energy, have the back straight, relax the jaws and relax the tongue. When the tongue is relaxed, it becomes harder to talk to ourself. It also gets nice and fat. Keeping it relaxed, press the tongue against the palate and breathe through the nose.

The Art and Heart of Ceremony

After you and your space are prepared, then what do you do? When your heart and mind are focused on why you are in your sacred space, and you have smudged your body, sacred items and space, then call in the helpful spirits. Some people drum, rattle, sing, ring bells, play a flute. Do whatever your tradition or heart calls you to do. These get the spirits' attention. Like attracts like via the vibrational pulse of spiritual reality. Use it to create sacred space that is both refuge to and outreach for the beneficent allies of the spirit world.

---

[5] Smudge yourself, smudge the space and smudge sacred items as much as desired. Smudge any time. Be mindful of smoke alarms though. Smudging can set them off, and nothing like a smoke alarm going off to ruin the mood. I will smudge my whole house from time to time, using whatever seems right at the moment. With a window or two open I go through every room, especially moving the stagnant energy out of every corner. I do doorways and doorknobs, too.

If you are there for some reason other than to say and offer thanks, I suggest following Wallace's advice for what he said to do when in the sweat lodge: simply ask for help and health. That's a great start. Let everything else flow from that, and then be receptive to changes within you and your space. Also be receptive to what happens at other times and places, because when sacred space becomes sacred space/time, outcomes of ceremonial actions can show up in surprising, but relevant, and magical ways. Whether you go into your sacred space to give thanks or to receive, it's a good idea to leave a physical offering.

A huge bonus of authentic ayni is that people develop true appreciation for the being and doing of others. I don't know how or why it works that way, but it does. Ayni can release pettiness and envy, taking great weight off body, mind and soul by evolving into a true appreciation of the talents and presence of others. It's probably because it is hard to approach these collective spiritual powers with a petty hearEveryone has artistic talent, a way to enhance or highlight the beauty of life for others. Being uninhibitedly authentic helps one develop art even more. When art comes from the heart, releasing it into the world of sacred space as ceremonial reciprocity is one of the strongest strands of the web connecting us to Spirit. Some say that's because inspiration – spirit is the root of the word – comes from Spirit, the Source, so returning a portion of our handiwork to creation renews the cycle.

Heart art, kitchen art, home art, garden art, food art, rock art, word art, music, dance and more are big hits with the spirits. Most physical objects left with the right intent that can degrade relatively soon are appropriate. Some people send plant offerings to the water, or burn or bury offerings so there is no smell to attract animals. Many offerings can be burned easily in a backyard fire pit. The medicine man Rolling Thunder once collected some plants, but had no tobacco to leave in return. So he left a few coins. For years I sliced my hand in exchange for cutting a Christmas tree out of the woods. Now I leave tobacco and smudge. People offer coffee, teas they blend, homebrew, herbal infusions and libations, seeds, nuts, flowers, fruits, vegetables they've grown or a little meat or fish they've dried. Others give time, beads, jewelry, small baskets, weavings, writings, cookies, brownies, a carving, painting, or a song, as did the Little Drummer Boy. Every culture has a mode of giving back. Every one of us can, too.

Having a sacred place or two or more in the home and yard welcomes magical spiritual energy. In many cultures, the home altar or kitchen is a focal point of the home. In American homes, it is often the entertainment center. Dedicating places to reverence, respect and reciprocity is a great family affair. These places need to be cared for and certainly can include the outdoor fire area, if that's possible.

Sacred space is mobile and becomes an ally in and of itself. It can be wherever you are. It is a container of creation. Right body, mind, heart, spirit and the intent to give back for everything received, sanctifies it. You do not need an altar or sacred items to create sacred space. Smudging and intent work fine. Don't be surprised if sacred objects come to you, though. When they do, sense their energy. Ask how to take care of and how to use them.

When I give offerings at home, I usually put them in a bowl for that purpose. I may hold the offering in my hands to imbue it with thanks, complementing the intent I added as I made it. I say thanks out loud, maybe do more smudging and music or prayer, then sit quietly, allowing the energy of reciprocity and appreciation to energize the space that holds me and totally release what I offer into the cosmos. After awhile, I again thank the allies and spirits who have helped me. I close the ceremony by singing a thank you song or saying "So mote it be," or, "*Aho! Mitake oyasin,*" which is a Lakota way of thanking all our relations. I clap my hands to let the spirits know I am complete, and then cleanup. Clapping the hands is also known to seal a ceremonial command or intent.

As for the offering, I may leave it in the bowl for a while, then burn it in a sacred fire later; sometimes I bury it. The intent is to allow spirits to consume the energy of the offerings. If I bring sage and flowers to a stream, I likely toss the flowers and sage ashes to help purify the water. Yep, I toss ashes into the water, which maybe amount to a couple of thimblefuls. Energetically, the flower and ash help protect the water through everything it will be subjected to as it flows away and into irrigation ditches and crops, toilets, golf courses, swimming pools, people, livestock, bathtubs, kitchen sinks and water treatment plants on its way to the sea.

There are many sacred libations, smudges and other offerings available. Learning them and learning to use them respectfully helps one center into the ayni of life. If you have a traditional lineage or are interested in your ancestry, discovering what was used as incenses and offerings is a good way to bring the past into the present. Almost every tradition has elaborate ceremonies and feasts by which to bring sacred reciprocity into practical connection with everyday life. What is offered here is a start of things you can incorporate into what feels right for you, as well as to provide some meaning of why and how certain ceremonial rites are done. You can't do anything wrong when your heart is open and give sincere thanks. Ceremony amplifies impact because of the positive energetic relationships created and shared. Pay attention. Be mindful. Be present. Be respectful and happy. Don't be worried about doing something wrong. Spirits are not nearly as petty as we are. When we do ayni authentically and consistently, mystery and magic come to us. Mystery loves company.

Within the crucible of sacred space, heart-felt ayni is a catalyst of karmic metamorphosis. Karma is complex and pervasive, so I won't pretend to address it. Anyone can find volumes about it in current and ancient texts. Even the Buddha acknowledged there is more at work and play in the course of human lives than a pure mechanistic existence determined by karma. Higher awareness and resultant higher action for the highest and greatest good does satisfy karma through harmonizing the vibrational state, if we are authentic. That is, authentic actions resonate on the soul level and beyond. Our evolution is still the natural result of karmic influences, which are not meant to punish or reward, but simply to comply with the vibrational state. So-called bad karma may indeed be satisfied when a person begins to function at a higher level of energy. This means moving up the scale of fear to love or metaphorically, from hell to heaven. Ayni catalyzes karma into a logical reaction of attraction based on our current rather than past states of consciousness. Hence, karma mutates. Rather than replicating the "Ghost of Experience Past," a catalyzed karmic sequence of evolutionary experience occurs. It is only logical, as Spock would say, that if our genes mutate, so can our karma. Through karmic mutation we re-member. That means a new memory occurs as we develop a new branch on our personal evolutionary tree, nourished by a composted understanding of the past. Our Aha! Moments and epiphanies crystallize the revelation of our personal apocalypses, so that what once was hidden is now seen. The shot of endorphin the brain gives itself is not just the reward of an epiphany. Like reciprocity, it is a catalyst that furthers our understanding, making a higher vibration possible. Evolution is the reward. It activates potential. This is covered more thoroughly in the last chapter.

Sacred space is built upon a foundation. Let's look at it by way of analogy of a house. A house has a foundation built upon principles of good building. It has a specific purpose, which is to hold up the rest of the building and create a buffer between the inside and outside worlds, and between the upper and lower worlds. The foundation of sacred reciprocity is much the same, although it can be dynamic. Based on your principles, it holds up everything else and can reduce the shock and awe of life. Gratitude and giving back is where it all begins after one becomes conscious of receiving or, I should say, becomes a conscious receiver.

Jack Schwarz was fond of saying, "A lower energy cannot penetrate a higher energy." I haven't found an actual law that confirms that, but intuitively it makes sense. Keep in mind that negative energy can be extremely powerful and can bring down positive energy with less amplitude, less power. Ayni establishes and maintains an aware connection between the inner and outer worlds and, at the same time, creates a healthy buffer between them. In other words, ayni acts like a semipermeable membrane. It lets in to sacred space what is beneficial and can keep out what is not.

Ayni is also foundation maintenance. It tends to repair chinks and daily wear and tear as it increases the awareness – even the awesomeness, a word I don't use often – of the connections between states of being and becoming, of giving and receiving. Giving back assures living forward.

If your rituals, your magic or you ever seem stagnant rather than dynamic, mix things up. In a constantly transforming universe, pay attention to your foundation. Allow everything to be in a state of motion of being and becoming, of expansion and contraction. We don't have to be like the woman whose daughter always cut her pot roasts in half and put them in separate pans before she put them in the oven. One day her husband asked her why she did that. She answered, "Because that's the way my mother did it." The next time the husband saw his mother-in-law, he asked her why she cut her pot roasts in half. She laughed and said, "Oh, I only did that once because I didn't have a roasting pan big enough for the whole thing."

Have fun with it! Sacred space isn't serious space. It's more like

Sirius Space, star space.

How does ayni increase our awareness? Paradoxically, by doing it without expecting anything in return. Be present, not in judgment or expectation, but in appreciation and support. Ask yourself why you give thanks. Ask yourself why you give back. Ask yourself why you appreciate. Ask yourself why you wonder. What amazes you? If answers come to you that deepen your appreciation for life through ayni and its reciprocity, those answers may lead to a greater awareness and sensitivity. With greater awareness of reciprocity, joy begins to flow through that semi-permeable membrane from all directions. Don Juan told Carlos Castaneda to balance the wonder of being alive with the terror of being alive. In light of Carlos' exaggeration and fabrication, who knows what don Juan actually said, but the world can seem to swing back and forth between the endorphin high of wonder and the adrenaline rush of "what the hell is going on?" Ayni smooths the ping-pong game of the life through its calming influence on us. I do enjoy a good game of ping-pong, though.

Everything is watching and everything is always listening. Being heard is another powerful benefit of sacred reciprocity. In a time when it seems to be harder and harder to be heard, spirits not only see us, they hear us and they understand.

7

Urban Ayni

When I run after what I think I want,
My days are a furnace of distress and anxiety;
If I sit in my own place of patience,
What I need flows to me,
And without any pain.

From this I understand that
What I want also wants me,
Is looking for me
And attracting me;
When it cannot attract me
Any more to go to it,
It has to come to me.

There is a great secret
In this for anyone
Who can grasp it.

– Rumi

Early in the initial Star Wars trilogy, Obi Wan Kenobi asked Yoda if he, Obi Wan, could train Luke Skywalker to become a Jedi. Yoda was against it. He said he had watched Luke for a long time. Scowling, he poked Luke with his stick and said Luke paid no attention to where he was or to what he was doing. It seems this type of behavior began a long time ago far, far away.

Luke lacked mindfulness. He lacked the ability to immerse himself in the here and now. Instead he chose discontent and distraction. Luke's unfocused and unsettled mind was a threat to himself – and the galaxy. Yoda knew what sort of disaster this inchoate material could create if it developed without the tempering qualities of mindfulness. Mindfulness is pure presence.

The universe is not a sporadic, fickle and conditional provider, so neither should be our reciprocity. To try to fetter the universe with prerequisites for how to satisfy our desires or meet our goals is mindless. Mindfulness helps us know what to ask for, how to ask for it, and how to use the creative flow for our fulfillment. Most importantly, mindfulness is the proper state of mind and heart for giving back. The less ego and the more heart in mindfulness, the better it is received, because the authentic heart puts more energy into the etheric field than does the unfocused mind.

While it might be easy to let the busyness and business of life impede the lack of focus and stillness of mind, the choice to live in the magic and fullness of the moment is always present. Imagine a Grand-Prix driver without mindfulness, who paid no attention to where he was or what he was doing. A driver not tuned in to every change in the road and to the traffic around him would not reach his goal. Nor would he be popular with the other drivers. If he lived long enough, he'd be kicked off the circuit.

The universe, however, is omni-patient. It hasn't kicked me off the circuit, no matter how many times I crash. It does not force me to change. It doesn't even force me to get a new vehicle – a physical body – and keep racing, but here I am again.

Patience is a key to and benefit of mindfulness. It provides access to the nonjudgmental and timeless nature of the universe. Patience coexists with peace. Hand-in-hand they lead to productive self-reflection, a meditative state where one can view and test, without emotional attachment, the appropriateness and consequences of the past and contemplate actions for the future. Peace through patience allows us to experience the Universal Mind. It may even allow the universe to experience ours, as inner and outer realities harmonize. For me, that harmony fosters the most appropriate mind-body state of mindfulness and action for any present-time situation.

Paradoxically, sometimes patience is right action. It's a perfect time to let the dough rise and go on to something else for a while. Patience is a perfect time for "corn and potatoes," to quote don Oscar. Or for the Buddhist to "chop wood and carry water." It is a perfect state of mind during our cosmic down time of rest and recreation, and as we go about fulfilling our daily needs and purpose.

The more relaxed and knowing we are, the more likely our desired outcome is manifested, provided clarity and intensity of feeling are present with right action. Getting up out of a chair and walking across the room is not a conscious thought. It is an intended action. And it happens. We don't need to be a Type A personality to get up and walk. Effortless effort allows the desired intent to happen. Ayni is the right action of right relationship. That's its purest intent, and the actions we take toward it imbue our entire life with balanced, responsive giving and receiving. The certain inner stillness required for right action is like the opposite of ripples made from tossing a stone in the water. By aligning proper movement, the ripples reverse, come to center and make the stone.

As we get even with the universe, manifestation occurs by things, from things, and for things acting in harmony with their own nature. Mindfulness creates the internal and external environments that enable us to see how intent manifests in infinitesimal and infinitely large ways. A plan in conflict with the creative flow can manifest, but that's the hard way. It requires constant attention, energy and management. There is no interactive creative thought to correlate the facets of activity into a naturally cohesive thrust into manifestation. If we don't know what to do, sacred space is a great place to ask for help and answers.

Living within an urban environment of environmental deprivations, denigrations, and degradations breeds a unique madness of self-destruction. It's as if the built environment is a Hydra. It stretches its reach by cutting off its own heads, growing two for each one cut, just to keep feeding itself. Examples are outside of the purview of this writing, but observe things for yourself to determine if it holds truth for you. Heracles finally killed the mythical Hydra terrorizing the countryside by cauterizing her cut off heads before new ones could grow. Then he cut off the central, immortal head and buried it under a heavy rock. Supposedly, that was the end of that.

I'm not so sure.

It's tough to pull off sacred reciprocity with the natural world in an urban environment and with an urban lifestyle. Cities and the urban lifestyle almost obliterate the natural world, although they are completely dependent upon natural processes, of course. There are international "sand wars" now because of the high demand for sand for concrete so we can keep building[6]. Beaches, islands and fishing grounds are being decimated by dredgers pulling up ocean sand. With the natural world out of reach and sight, it becomes more difficult for many who live in an urban area to find a spiritual connection through frequent sacred reciprocity. Killing the planet will make it impossible.

Friends help each other. Good friends enjoy helping each other. There is reciprocity. Respect, admiration, acknowledgement, giving and receiving and doing things together are appreciated and build the bonds of friendship more strongly. The same is true with the natural and unseen worlds. Sacred reciprocity builds bonds of life for life. Doesn't our modern behavior toward and relationship with the natural world seem odd considering it provides us at least as much as do family and friends? Because of how it balances relationship, ayni supports sacred space. That sacred space becomes an alchemist's cauldron of potential and a crucible of transformation. It also brings a sense of harmony and balance, often missing from modern life.

Chief Seattle purportedly said, "The Earth does not belong to us. We belong to the Earth." Imagine relaxing into this kind of belonging. It takes off a lot of pressure. To belong means to be in relationship, "bound to and by ties of affection." Most of us have a tie to the planet and the beauty here. We love our home, where we grew up, our family and friends and favorite places. It takes work to sustain these relationships, and affection to grow them. Like a plant, we wither when pulled

---

[6] From the PBS.org description of the documentary titled *Sand Wars*: Sand is one of the most consumed natural resources on the planet. As a raw material, it is of huge importance to the building and construction industry – indeed, houses, skyscrapers, bridges, airports, and pavements are all partially composed of sand. Melted and transformed into glass, it features in every window. It is also the source of silicon dioxide, a mineral found in our wines, cleaning products, cosmetics and an astounding variety of other products that we use on a daily basis. As demand rises in an increasingly industrialized world, however, the planet's reserves of sand are coming under threat. It is estimated that three quarters of the world's beaches are in decline and likely to disappear. Such is the demand for the material that sand has even attracted the attention of the criminal fraternity, who have taken to plundering beaches and rivers for what is becoming a prized commodity.

from loving connection whether from family or the earth.

Years ago, I studied environmental and experiential education and led outdoor education programs. It was posited that the benefits from an outdoor experience usually, but not always, lasted only as long as the experience did. That means if a person had a three-week wilderness experience, the transformational impact of that experience lasted about three weeks before the person returned "to normal." The impact time varies, though.

I've seen young people hate being in nature and who never felt comfortable there, especially if parents or a judge ordered them to an outdoor rehab program. Others would try to dominate their new surroundings, sometimes out of fear. Others fell in love with almost everything and did not want to go home. Some participants say they had a lasting transformation or an epiphany. For these people, a quest begins for a return to nature, a return to spirit and reclamation of their power and purpose. Regardless of our situation in life, many see this return as the inevitable path of humanity, our return to Source through our conscious evolution predicated by the evolution of the planet. However, without involving cities in reciprocities, many who share our common human experience will continue to have their energies adulterated, and we see plenty of weird ways that is expressed. What can be done? How to do ayni in a city?

Cities that are more livable are more reciprocal. Cities include rooftop gardens, parks and trails, street trees, falcon perches, renewable energy sites, earth-friendly manufacturing, courtyards, fountains and "green" architecture. Any of these can become sacred space for reciprocity – but don't disturb the falcons. Two good places to say thank you are the drinking water treatment and wastewater treatment plants. However, the private outdoor natural sanctuary often sought for reciprocity can be difficult to find in a city, so there are ways to bring it about. An ayni oasis can be fostered anywhere. Individual altars of reciprocity reflect the inner world. Once we realize we not only attract magic, but are magic, things change. We see the indomitability of life and spirit.

We can extend random acts of kindness into random acts of reciprocity. When a plant grows in a crack of a sidewalk or a building, it uses every nanogram of its beingness to bring life into the city. Thank that plant. Acknowledge it. Water it. There are other ways. Get a bird feeder, a birdbath, wind chimes, a water fountain. Give blessings to a rooftop garden. We can also leave libation, a thimbleful of spirits to the nature spirits in a park, for example. Smudge wherever we can. Bless the water when we shower, when we drink, when we flush the toilet, maybe as we keep in mind the insanity of soiling potable water. Invest in renewable energy, which is also human energy, and energy conservation.

Trees are among the greatest remedies to offset degradations foisted upon the natural world and the human psyche. More and more information is being documented about that. Matthew Silverstone's book *Blinded by Science*, documents research that confirms the beneficial effects of trees on people. What's the best thing people can do for a maximum positive effect? Hug a tree.[7]

Trees are literal and figurative portals to other worlds. Unfettered beings in a world of squares, boxes, straight lines, barriers and private land ownership, trees extend a feeling of what it is like to be and to be a tree. They are a portal and bridge between the Three Worlds – the Above, the Physical and the Below. This is how our pagan ancestors saw them. Symbolically, their branches extend to the heavens above, into the realm of light, higher thought, revelation and creativity; their trunk represents our physical life and body and steadfastness; their roots travel into the below, into the richness of our subconscious and unconscious mind, and dreams, daemons and altered states. To thank a tree, all we need to do is extend our consciousness and appreciate them. By blending with their awareness, we calm down and get grounded, making connections with other entities, beings and dimensions more possible. Trees live in the eternal present, which may be the greatest of all the gifts they give. Their growth rings emulate the Akashic records and the information therein, and universal expansion. Consummate artists of reciprocity, they give food, fuel, shelter and shade, purify air and water, build and hold the soil, and sanctify space. Trees have energy fields comparable to ours, so we can develop great relationships with them. Great relationship and sacred space go hand in hand.

Because of their actual and metaphorical connection to the Three Worlds, trees are an avenue of mystical freedom. When we tune in to their vibration and their consciousness, they carry away our conscious-

[7] The HeartMath Institute is researching the tree hugging phenomenon, too.

ness to altered states. Through them we can learn, witness and unravel mysteries of self, time and connections. How? Refine experiencing a tree. Take it one leaf at a time when the wind blows. When we see how each and every leaf has a different pattern of movement and of vibration, we can begin to hear the movement of the leaves and branches, not as just movement in the wind, but as music of the spheres. It is like watching a concert pianist's fingers on a piano keyboard. This effect cannot be experienced easily from the ground. It's much easier to witness looking out a 2nd, 3rd story or 4th story window, but it's best to climb a tree and get even with the branches swaying in the wind, although looking up from a hammock can be very nice.

I live in a TreeHouse. There is a large city tree outside my home office window. I smudge her. I water her. If I don't get water to her soon enough, she lets me know. Over the years, when the other neighborhood trees have been stressed and droopy brown during summer drought, her leaves are lush and branches supple. I water her deeply at night. I wonder if anyone wonders how she stays that way in the heat of long summer. I do know if people would water their trees instead of their lawns, both lawns and trees and people would be in better shape. The energy in the neighborhood would be better, too, with happy instead of thirsty trees. So smudging under a full moon and conscious watering develop the attentiveness the TreeHouse tree and I have to one another. Our relationship has built over time. It takes time, intent and action to build and maintain a loving relationship. So be patient with trees and whatever you approach in the natural world, and know it might take time to get a reciprocal response.

I need to get a little scientific again to make a point. People evolved within a very subtle, but powerful electric field known as the Schumann Resonance...a pulsing of earth-based rhythms measuring approximately 7.83 cps or 7.83 Hertz (Hz). Coincidentally, this happens to be the same predominant rhythm brain waves are at when we are in the alpha state, the state of relaxation and mind-body regulation and so-called peak performance. The breathing pattern offered earlier is proven to get people into alpha. The key to this statement is that this is the "predominant" pattern. That means the other brain wave states are there, too...lambda, hyper gamma, gamma, beta, alpha, alpha-theta,

theta, theta-delta, delta, epsilon and likely others too subtle to detect.[8]

This frequency, and its harmonics at 14, 20, 26, 33, 39 and 45 Hz, form Schumann Resonances. What keeps this field pulsing is lightning. Lightning strikes the earth approximately 100 times a second. This ongoing electrical storm creates a standing wave of electromagnetism from the surface of the earth to about 55 miles up to the ionosphere. All life has evolved within this electromagnetic cocoon, which includes weaker geomagnetic waves from within the planet. This suggests that ancient claims that mankind depends on two subtle energies, the yin/female energy from below and the yang/male energy from above, are right. Good sacred space has both. The human brain and body seem to share many relationships with this energetic envelope. Science, medicine and other disciplines know living bodies are electromagnetic, so all of us have developed within this cocoon of lightning-made electromagnetism. Manmade electrical fields permeating the environment via transmission towers of all kinds and frequencies, as well as buildings wrapped in wiring for 60 Hz current, in which we now spend the majority of our lives, are a suspect in exacerbating, if not causing, mental maladies such as depression, anxiety and migraines. In other words, there has been some research studying whether or not manmade environments are overriding the natural electromagnetic cocoon to our detriment. Cell phones are one of the prime suspects. I encourage the reader to check into these findings, if interested. On the other hand, it may mean we just need to spend more time outside.

The point of this is not to discuss the pros and cons of Schumann resonance-based products, which serve as a focal point for skeptics bent on undermining the importance of our evolutionary electromagnetic field, but rather to emphasize our connection with the natural world and suggest why our ancestors considered lightning to be either a god or a tool of the gods. And it may explain my passion for catching lightning bugs on summer nights and dressing up as Thor on Hallowe'en.

On one hand, it seems obvious why our distant ancestors would fear lightning and attribute it to the gods. On the other hand, some cultures claim the most powerful shamans are those who have been called by the Thunder Beings. This means they have been hit by light-

[8] An excellent chart of brain waves and their characteristics can be seen at www.infiniteminds.info.

ning. As Nan Moss wrote in the book *Weather Shamans:* "So, Thunder beings are dangerous, but protectors and givers of power, reflecting the inherent duality of the world." (Sounds like a jaguar.) Because of the importance of lightning and our ancestors' awareness of its connection to the planet, it is no wonder indigenous cultures have paid homage to such deities. Lightning also seems to repair the Earth's ozone layer, a side effect we should welcome.

Knowledge is power. As we cordon ourselves off from the planet's vibratory state, are we really willing to dismiss the possibility that we are cutting ourselves off from power? Are we creating an energetic environment in which human capability is diminished or interfered with, thereby requiring the excessive and imposing use of technology for us to function and communicate? And is it really impossible for us to develop advanced technologies in-tune with life? To the final question I have to answer I don't think so. I do feel we seldom hear the whispers of natural powers, let alone act upon them. Super storms and climate change and our many challenges are not punishments, but some may be the result of us forgetting how to keep sacred space as the sacred space from which we evolved, as it was conducive to hearing some very helpful things, including our intuition. The anti-Faraday cage wrapped around every home and building – and increasingly in the outdoor environment – screens us from accepting downloads from the surrounding energetic field, generated and maintained by lightning. When a breath held in sacred pause within our sacred space is released as an *om* that raises the ohm of the vibrational frequencies of the anti-Faraday cages in which we live, we counteract the ohm of resistance and enter the flow of Om.

The sun and lightning were looked at as sources of power, which means information. Today we hide from the sun and run from lightning. I'm not advocating sunburn and lightning strikes, but when we shield ourselves from these natural sources of energy by living too much in buildings, we may need to do something to balance our lifestyle. Maya elder Hunbatz Men suggests, "... pray to the Sun, the cosmos, because the Sun will wake up your memory."

Regarding these challenges, there is conjecture that there is no need to worry. Some say the positive evolutionary changes are anchored and the planet will survive. That may be true. The flow of creation toward its Source is unstoppable. And yet, it is mutable and malleable. The choice between fear and love remains. If we choose fear, fear won't stop the flow, but it will alter our experience within it, stymieing us in eddies, and spinning us from whirlpools into cesspools. Fear can create repetitious experience spanning many lifetimes. It feeds the ego not the spirit and soul. Stagnation and repetition may create the density of consciousness that makes change on our planet so recalcitrant and difficult.

Love won't keep us out of trouble. Love is trouble. Anyone with a lover or in love knows that. Love is the panacea for what ails us, though. All we have to do is choose it. Love opens things to the light of day and whatever other light might be on the way. Love can transform a whirlpool into a merry-go-round, a cesspool into fountain, a compost pile into a garden, an eddy into a sanctuary of self-reflection. Through love, ayni is reciprocated and through ayni love is received. Ultimately love, in its many facets and forms and expressions, is understood through non-attached giving and receiving. Without love or true reverence and presence, there is no ayni; there is only an offering. The subtle energies and seen and unseen presences with which we deal sense our commitment and respond, or don't, in a reciprocated manner. When we are true, when we are present, when we are reverent, when we are intent and sincere, the ayni we offer does alter our reality in benevolently inexplicable ways, feeding our childlike amusement and satisfying our curiosity as we step back, let go and witness how the universe actually does provide for us. It takes trust, right action and being true to oneself.

Knowledge plus experience lead to wisdom. Wisdom connects us with the environment. One reason apprenticeships of mystery schools were so intense and involved is to assure the adept did not abuse his or her ability to inappropriately influence the environment and outcomes. Inappropriate influence is the product of ego and ignorance. Standards seem significantly lower today, allowing the woefully and willfully untrained to regulate the common wealth and common conscious contained within the common sacred space of our planet. Mother Earth could use some love.

Another way to improve our sacred relationships is to hold ourselves in higher esteem than do "economic indicators." Years ago, people were not as smart as we are today. Artisans did not know how to make things that did not last. So, their customers were referred to as...customers. This implies what was bought and sold was custom-made, to the buyer's specifications and needs. This added quality, service, utility and longevity. Reputations were built upon what was built and how well it was built.

We are now consumers. There is a Consumer Price Index, but no Customer Relationship Index. A customer has a totally different connotation than a person who is merely a consumer. In a time of seemingly more limited resources, being a customer rather than a consumer is a practice of self-care, of using one's power to assert a relationship by consciously acknowledging the connection with all that sustains our life and livelihood and the planet.

Many factors contribute to things being mass-produced today. When it became more important for goods and services to be consumed rather than custom-made, our appreciation for what we received went down. Rather than being appreciative, we began to spend our time working more to buy more because what we had wore out too soon. Now the planet is populated with generations of consumers rather than customers. We talk about consumerism, but *customerism* is not a word. Why not? Because we aren't supposed to talk about it?

Despite how often the word artisan is used for what we buy today, we are surrounded by inferior quality, which makes heartfelt gratitude more difficult. Sources and resources should not be used to make crap. In other words, the emperor wearing no clothes would be infinitely better than what he is actually wearing. To deny the emperor wears crappy clothes is to deny any truth when we are faced with overwhelming evidence, yet refuse to believe or act upon any of it. Being authentic, so important to creating and being with sacred space, requires that individual truth is acted upon.

Sociologists have convinced marketers that people are more likely to move away from pain than toward something beneficial. Is pain the same as fear? Is love the same as a benefit? Why are we more likely to move away from something painful than toward something beneficial? I doubt if this is true for everyone. I sense it is true for those who still move predominantly out of fear than love. Maybe consumers are the fear-based market, buying stuff to momentarily move away from their dollars and doldrums. Customers are the love-based market, moving toward value and discernment, an appreciation of craftsmanship, materials and utility. Of course customers consume, but that is not their purpose. Customers may have a greater discerning perception of the intrinsic value and purpose of what they consume. Hence, the rarity of commodity and its craftsmanship ties the customer to the raw material, which is the natural world from whence the item came, intrinsically creating a stronger bond and symbiosis, and so creates appreciation and relationship. Do not invite fear into sacred space by bringing it in. Customize it to the highest possible vibration.

Here's an ayni story from one of my revered shamanic brothers. It shows how to customize family space and memory.

ADIRONDACK APACHETA BY PIETER LEFFERTS

My family has a camp in the Adirondack Mountains in upstate New York. It's off the grid, about ten miles from civilization and is accessible only by rowing two lakes with a mile hike between them. We have real beds, running water, hot showers and full indoor plumbing plus a propane powered refrigerator and cook stove so while we're miles from cars, phones and electricity, camp life is comfortable, freed from the trappings of the outside world.

I've been going to camp for over fifty years. My great uncle Hal and his wife Betsy had camp built in 1933. They were quite the couple. Hal had a ready wit and Betsy would tell us kids ghost stories before leaving us to our fear of what goes bump in the night. They were old school, proper folk. Cocktails were ritual and in a sense carried over to the proclaiming of 'It's a gin clear day!' meaning ideal weather for a mountain climb or daylong canoe trip. They loved their quiet time in camp, content with knowing the flock was off gallivanting for the day. My parents took over stewardship of camp in the late 1960s.

When Hal died in 1975, it was Betsy's wish that his ashes be scattered within the embrace of his beloved retreat. So one August day there was a small gathering of his wife, Betsy, their daughter Cynthia, or Cynnie as she was known, my parents and a few of Hal's contemporaries. I was the sole representative of the third generation, at 18 years old. My father chose a glen of young spruce for the ceremony, just off the footpath to the single room cabin where in my earliest visits Hal and Betsy stayed, and then were succeeded by my parents. It's known as the Palais Royale, fit for the King and Queen. My father also asked me how I felt about finding a stone from Crystal Brook, our water source, as a simple marker for Hal's return to the good earth. It was a natural task for me. I hopped from stone to stone eyeing the stones in the stream until 'the one' spoke to me. It's an early memory of my intuitive self, one that I recognize with hindsight as being nurtured by my many years in close relationship with nature, an inner voice built on trusting the message of the heart, or, in other words, what feels right. Since that day I've provided three more stone memorials, for Betsy a few years later, Cynnie in 2009, and most recently my father, Farnham, who died in 2013.

I've tended the sanctuary for forty years, regularly clearing leaves and sitting in silent contemplation. So it was only natural that I would locate a sacred cairn, or apacheta as it's known in the Andes, as an addition to the sanctuary. I learned about apachetas from my teacher, don Oscar Miro-Quesada. An apacheta is an energetic connection to Pachamama, Mother Earth, and is a living entity in its own right honoring the spirits of the mountains, the *apus*, of where the apacheta is located. With permission, guidance and blessings of the spirits and Spirit, the apacheta ceremony begins. Building an apacheta starts with selecting twelve directional stones surrounding a center foundation stone. Before the stones are placed, the ground upon which the apacheta will be built is consecrated with offerings of a clear spirit libation, such as Florida Water, along with cornmeal, tobacco and a special three-leaf *kintu*[9] placed in the center. Over the course of the summer of 2014 I gathered stones, several as large as I could maneuver single-handedly. I cleared the duff from where the apacheta was to be built and lined up my 'stone relatives' along the path to the sanctuary where they sat until I was ready for ceremony. That day would come at the end of the season for trips to camp.

September is a beautiful month in the north woods. Warm days and chilly nights, marked with the rise of Orion, bring a sense of industry to time in the woods. I spent a week that fall making repairs to buildings, cutting, splitting and stacking wood, alongside my brother, Marshall. One morning as we got to work I said to him, "We're going to see a bear today. The bear is coming through." After many years and many bears I've developed a sense for when a bear is in the neighborhood. Marsh knows me to be right most of the time. We finished our

[9] In Peruvian culture, a three-leaf kintu is made of cocoa leaves. In the States and elsewhere, a kintu is often made with bay leaves.

work for the day.

It was my night to cook, but beforehand I enjoyed a cocktail on the dock with our dinner guest, Adam. The day was slipping into evening when I left Adam with Marsh at the dock while I went to build the cook fire and prep dinner. I laid the fire but before lighting it I decided I would visit the site of the apacheta. I'd offer the open ground a drink of Florida Water as a toast to things to come. Somehow 'the ground' seemed thirsty to me, too. I walked the path in the dusk and turned the corner by the cabin. There in front of me stood the bear! I called to the others to come look as the bear passed through. 'Nice affirmation,' I thought as I went back to making dinner. But I had forgotten to offer the small libation, just a drop of Florida Water, a kiss upon the open earth! 'The spirits are thirsty,' I told myself.

It was still light enough to see and, after all, the bear had come and gone. I planned to dash to the site and make the offering with plenty of time to get dinner done before dark. Up the trail I went. I rounded the corner of the cabin with the impression of the bear fresh in my mind, but he was not there. There was only stillness in a sea of ferns in the fading light. I continued on the path to the Palais Royale and took the left turn to The Sanctuary. The spruce are tall there, forming a forest cathedral, an intimate cove to commune with my ancestors. I crouched low to the ground over the earthen ring, the footprint of the apacheta. I opened the bottle of Florida Water feeling reverent, glad to be showing up with a heartfelt exchange between nature seen and unseen. I tilted the bottle sideways, ready to release the sacred drop into the waiting mouths of the elemental nature spirts, eager for the taste. But I halted. Something was wrong; something did not feel right. Florida Water felt foreign, exotic and curiously out of place at the moment. I hemmed and I hawed. I screwed the cap back on the bottle and stood up.

'What am I feeling?' I asked myself. 'Why am I hesitant, even resistant? Will I offend don Oscar, if I decline to follow his prescription for sacred consecration?' There is ritual, yes, he would want me to understand. And there is following your heart. That he would wholeheartedly endorse. I looked around the woods. Nightfall was filling in the gaps. I turned to my relatives: Hal, Betsy, Cynnie and my father. I laughed out loud! "Haha! They're gin drinkers!" I said with delight. I could hear them, their ancestral chorus calling to me from beyond the veil.

"What on earth were you thinking?" they wanted to know. "Remember us!"

"I understand. I get it and I will go get it. I'll be right back." I told them.

"Thank God you'll do it right!" I felt them exclaim.

I returned with a bottle of gin, clear as an Adirondack day. I knelt to Pachamama. I took off the cap. I offered to the open ground a libation free of doubt or reticence, with the fullness of my heart. I trusted my inner voice as one in sacred reciprocity with the voices of my ancestors, the apus, the elementals.

The next day I completed my apacheta building ceremony under a bright sky. I chanted in Quechua as I adorned the stones with leaves of flame red maple and golden beech. I bade it temporary farewell; this was the last trip of the season. Winter would soon blanket it in deep snow. I could only imagine its presence until the following spring. I've made more apachetas since my Adirondack Apacheta, even another for my father at his home, consecrated with a gin libation as well. But for others I have used Florida Water. It works just fine.

~~~~~~~~~~~~~~~~~~~

As Pieter's story shows, ayni can be a personal or family affair. It's a good practice to revisit places you or your family hold dear, and express how and why you honor them. If you do it only from your mind and heart within your personal sacred space, that's great, too. Ayni can also be a group, school, business or community effort. For example, schools can do something to enhance the habitat of their school mascot. This is seldom done. How many colleges and universities are leaders in preserving the habitat of their animal ally/mascot? What would this do? Nurture a true bond of sanctity and reciprocity and help assure a place on the planet for so much more than us, or anger potential donors because a school supported its mascot's inclusion in environmental protection? I'm not sure, but this could have great potential to build school spirit and connect with Spirit.

A book club may want to do an outside offering for the public library, but I don't recommend a book burning. Businesses could give back to the resource to which they are most indebted, as well. For instance, Caterpillar Tractor could increase its commitment to sustainability by helping preserve monarch butterflies. Geico Insurance could
~~~~~~~~~~~~~~~~~~~

support habitat for endangered geckos.

When's the last time someone offered ayni to an oil well? A coal mine? A power plant? A lumber yard? The county dump? Sand? A rock quarry? A snowplow driver? The possibilities are endless. Each act of sacred reciprocity connects us with what sustains us, and boosts the energy of life and consciousness through right relationship.

8

Answers in the Fire

"There are two ways to be fooled. One way is to believe what is not true. The other is to refuse to believe what is."
Soren Kierkegaard

Because we share the awesome power and responsibility of co-creation, it is a good idea to apprentice with elders wise in the true ways of the world. Unfortunately, we may not often ask elders for guidance because we may think the world is so different for us than it was for them. That's true to an extent. Conversely, when asked for advice, some elders don't know how to respond. On the other hand, we may not know how to listen. Late in his years, I asked my dad to give me some great teaching, some great learning he gleaned from life – something to share with me before he passed. He simply said, "Well, ya gotta do something."

I had hoped for something more. 'That's it?' I thought.

Yet, upon deep and lengthy reflection, I realized he was right.

As mentioned, the Inca had three basic rules for community conduct. "Don't lie. Don't steal. Don't be lazy." As a matter of fact, an Inca could be executed for being lazy. It went against caring for the community and its sustainable welfare and longevity. Every Inca had to do something.

Do something. Those are empowering words.

Do something. Spontaneous or planned? Provocative or evocative? Evolutionary or revolutionary? Unitive or punitive? Transformative or divisive? Active or passive?

Had he said the same thing using different words, the effect may have been more immediate, instead of years in the making. For example, had he said, "Give back." "Follow your heart." Or something akin to the Incan sagacious trilogy of, "Don't lie. Don't steal. Don't be lazy." But he did not. I had to learn to do something myself.

As it is impossible to do anything without receiving, it seems impossible to receive without giving something in return.

A corollary of "Do something" is "Be true to yourself." Sometimes we have to be a human doing. Somewhere on the path of doing is also the opportunity to learn to be a full human being. Like so many things for optimal health and expression, a dynamic balance along a continuum should exist with these two states. Being when we need to be and doing when we need to do are the corn and potatoes, the chop wood and carry water, of life. They are the essential of what we need to do to be true to ourselves. Ayni reflects possible human beings and human doings for that balance. We are being grateful; we are doing gratitude. Be grateful. Do gratitude.

I moved to Ashland, Oregon in 1979 to do something. Ashland was home to South Oregon State College (SOSC, now known as Southern Oregon University). A year earlier, Wallace Black Elk came to town and looked up Dr. William Lyon, an anthropologist at SOSC. Basically, Wallace announced he would start leading sweat lodges in the area and invited Lyon's students to participate. Lyon took Wallace up on the offer and actually offered it as a college class. It later won first place in the North American Association of Summer Sessions Creative Program Award contest. This was about the time I met Lyon and Wallace.

Wallace was an amazing man and shaman. Southern Oregon is usually hot and dry during the late summer, and that summer was no exception. One hot August evening at his camp several miles outside of town, Wallace was watching a huge fire heating rocks for the night's sweat. There was a fire ban in place, so the large column of smoke was a give-away of an illegal burn. Soon, an official government truck with two men in it came roaring down the hill on the dirt road. It pulled up to the fire in a cloud of dust. The men got out.

One man yelled. "Put out that fire!"

Wallace, who spoke English very well, could also act as if he couldn't. From his chair under a tree, he simply said in somewhat halting words, "Sacred fire. Won't hurt anything."

The men plodded toward Wallace. "Put out that fire!" one hollered again.

Wallace smiled and quietly said, "Sacred fire. Won't hurt anything."

As threats, veiled threats and invectives flew, Wallace sat peacefully looking at the men. Despite the tension, everyone noticed it had suddenly gotten dark.

At the top of the smoke plume of the sacred fire where the smoke flattened out, a bird hovered. Some said it was a hawk; others said it was an eagle. In any case, as the bird flapped its wings, the top of the plume swirled into a gray-black donut-shaped circle.

It began to rain. Huge drops splattered straight down on everyone, but not on the fire, which was under the donut hole. The government men looked terrified. Wallace smiled. One quickly gave Wallace a fire permit. Then chased by the heavy smells of dust and rain, the men ran to their truck, drove back up the hill, never to be heard from again. And on top of all that, Wallace also got a fire permit, without having to go get one. It came to him.

Wallace smiled and said, "Sacred fire. Won't hurt anything."

It didn't. The rain soon stopped and Wallace poured a hot sweat that night.

Why tell you this? This is not really a book of shamanism although it relates to it. Is it just another anecdotal Indian story of instant gratification, a moment of amusement from the constant battles between cultures? Did it happen because Wallace simply could not take no for an answer? Probably not. I think there is more to it than that.

Wallace's effortless act of divine defiance without the histrionics of a rain dance or cloud seeding was the result of a lifetime of sacred reciprocity. As don Juan would say, Wallace's command became the Eagle's command. Wallace used to say his ways were not Indian ways. He said his ways were Earth Man ways. "If my ways were Indian ways, all the Indians would be doing them, but they're not," he said. Earth Man ways and magic go hand in hand.

Dictionary.com defines magic as "the art of producing a desired effect or result through the use of incantation or various other techniques that presumably assure human control of supernatural agencies or the forces of nature." With this definition, processes such as aerial cloud seeding could be considered magic, as it uses techniques that may produce the desired effect of rain through human control – or manipulation – of the forces of nature.

I think this is one of life's great lessons: magic is the inevitable result of the connective, reflexive and responsive cause-and-effect universe in which we live. Its evidence is everywhere. Why deny it? Maybe because if magic exists, we would have to consider that there is a consciousness out there that we do not recognize, control, perceive or understand. Science and magic may be polar counterparts to doing and being. It's not necessary to pick one over the other. I believe many people don't believe in magic because magic would make them vulnerable to those who use it. The thing is we're all magicians already and need to come out of the closet. The basic processes are the same whether one wants to put out a fire with an eagle or a sprinkler system. One imagines it, intends it and creates it.

Could someone else besides Wallace "make it rain" when officials threaten a sacred fire? Of course, and there are many comparable examples. Dr. William Lyon wrote about these extensively in his book *Spirit Talkers*[10]. Lyon said he accepts that science requires that if supernatural events cannot be scientifically explained, they cannot be declared real. He points out that that is only half of the story, and it's the other half science ignores. Lyon adds, "That part says that you cannot dismiss any observed phenomenon until you prove that it does not exist." Consequently, "there is no scientific proof that supernatural events do not occur." The reason for this is because they have been observed.

I might say, "Wallace made it rain," but is that true? Did he seed the clouds? The smoke? The result may have originated from his absolute trust in "Sacred fire. Won't hurt anything." It may have been Wallace's total trust in the fire, and the fire's reciprocity to Wallace,

[10] In his landmark book, *Spirit Talkers: North American Indian Medicine Powers*, Dr. William Lyon gives extensive examples of documented displays of shamanic powers witnessed by westerners, many of whom were credible scientists living with North American tribes.

that took the form of rain to demonstrate the fire's truth and trust in Wallace. In other words, maybe the fire made it rain.

You may ask, "That's great, but what good is it to make it rain? I don't plan to run a sweat lodge. And what if I do make it rain, but can't make it stop?"

The magic that shows up when you show up is frequently just for you. It resonates with you. In a conscious and connected universe the gifts are not like the socks you get every year for Christmas from your grandmother, nice as they may be. The gift is in the magical reciprocity of opening your world to greater awareness and consciousness. Imagine if you were only half as aware as you are now. Life would be duller with less energy coming in to stimulate you. Now imagine being twice as aware as you are now. That is the type of gift of magical reciprocity that can show up unexpectedly when a person offers heart-felt ayni. It may take the actual form of a greater awareness of cause and effect, such as rain falling around the sacred fire. Greater awareness, more appreciation and consciousness are often the initial gifts of magical reciprocity. Wallace knew what he had to do and be and intend for that. It's a gift for us to sense how to do the same.

So, what to do to stop the rain? Still yourself and simply ask *for* the rain to stop. This is much different than asking *the* rain to stop, which would mean the rain would stop itself. Subtle differences work well in the realm of subtle powers, differences so subtle they are impossible to miss. In other words, as I don't know what made it rain, I don't know what will make it stop. Asking for the rain to stop summons the rain stopper, which may or may not be the rainmaker.

Words are power, backed with intent and the breath of the Creator when we speak. Our intent. The Creator's breath. Directed action into sacred space. We speak our intent into sacred space using the Creator's breath, take right action and then let it all go. These are pieces of the co-creation puzzle. Magic happens when they all come together.

9

Being non-attached in a Connected Universe

"The mind is its own place, and in itself can make a heaven of hell, a hell of heaven."
John Milton – Paradise Lost

Jack Schwarz explained that his psychic and healing talents were due to his radiant energy from his high functioning state of health, not as the result of him being special or receiving gifts from outside forces. His said his health was a product of how he lived and his "knowing systems," rather than belief systems. Jack did not refer to himself as a shaman or guru, although he exhibited abilities often attributed to them. However, as he was studied in western research laboratories, he may have been more readily accepted by science than some of his mystic contemporaries, such as Rolling Thunder, whom Jack considered to be a fantastic medicine man.

What did the research facilities find out about Jack, a man who was fond of sticking stainless needles as large around as pencils through his arms without bleeding? A man who could heal those wounds as the needle was removed from his arm? What researchers found is that Jack was able to go into different brain wave states to achieve such body regulation, what he called voluntary controls. His mental state, breathing patterns and visualizations, as well as a sense of non-attachment from his body, were his part of his magic.

A Dutch Jew, Jack was imprisoned and tortured by the Nazis during WWII. As a teenager Jack was already well known as a healer before the Nazi occupation. The Nazis were enthralled by such things, knew of Jack and captured him. He later escaped. After the war, Jack was a research subject both in the U.S. and abroad. Some of the most rigorous studies were conducted at the Menninger Institute by a team led by Dr. Elmer Green, a well-respected scientist. Green then wrote a comprehensive book about his findings titled *Beyond Biofeedback*, published in 1977. Jack was a major part of this research, designed to discover how some people exhibited such extraordinary controls over their mind-body state. Among the discoveries about Jack is that when he did his needle through the arm trick, he did not block the pain. He and his body agreed they would do it together, hence, once that state of harmony was attained and maintained, there was no need to block pain because there was no pain. Pain is a signal to tell us we need to respond. If a mind-body action has been agreed upon, there is no need to get the pain signal. Such a state of nonattachment coincides with a state of being present.

While the 1970s were a time of scientific research to explore the human potential, the race to develop artificial intelligence and computer technology was on the cusp. In some ways this represents a split in our world view, one in which the human potential could thrive in conjunction with, but not abdicate to, technology, and the other where human potential was subordinate to technology and stymied by it. Sacred space and reciprocity are inherent in the former. In the latter, not so much. In Jack's opinion, health was immanently related to our state of consciousness. Both are states of energy. It is our responsibility to continually develop both states. He said radiant health and an evolving state of consciousness entail more refined and dynamic connections among our mental, emotional, physical and spiritual states. In addition, Jack said health is transformational, not static. He explained that a healthy mind-body was the optimal state we require to express our life's purpose. Thus, what might be healthy for me may not be healthy for you.

I don't think it's ever been documented that a high state of human consciousness is detrimental to human health, to the health of others or to the planet. More refined and greater mental-emotional-physical-spiritual connections enhance right relationship to sacred space and to technology. This is what connections do. They connect, integrate and elevate. Right relationship does not subordinate. In studies done on Jack and others, researchers discovered how these subjects did what they did. Whereas some modern technology seems to control what we think and experience and how we behave, other technology, such as that pioneered by Elmer Green's research and others, helps people learn how to achieve mind-body states conducive to attaining greater health and awareness. It helps us understand the importance of putting into play our diverse human potentials and connections with one another and the planet. In other words, this type of technology gives us help and health, and can support our work within sacred space.

However, some people with whom I talk believe that ceremony and appreciation, especially when offered to seen and unseen entities of nature, mean a return to a backward, superstitious and Luddite state. Not so. Sacred space, reciprocity and authenticity expand the human experience. One of the few things sacred space and ceremony do apprehend, though, is excessive self-importance. They don't censor it; they tend to shapeshift self-importance into a way of being that allows for the openhearted investigation of realities. Through this, sacred space and reciprocity bring about evolutionary growth and realization. When mind-body harmony is acquired, the way we use technology, or anything else, for that matter, is predicated upon service rather than avarice, and authenticity rather than duplicity. Mind-body harmony is like health in that it can be thought of as the most optimal and dynamic state to be in to accomplish what needs to be done in the moment. Paradoxically, it is also a state of non-attachment because we put our trust in the moment rather than a desired outcome based on our actions. Think of it like this: the moment is always more than our actions.

The attainment of non-attachment, which is itself a paradox, is one of the most sought after states of conscious evolution, but what does it have to do with magic? Quite a bit. The bond of everything to everything is strengthened by intent and knowing what to do when, if anything. Living this paradox leads one into a greater involvement with energy beyond the physical. Non-attachment does not mean we are not connected to the universe and to everything, although the word may suggest that. That's detachment, which is a problem, not an answer.

Non-attachment is an aspect of letting go. It means we act without expecting reward and without attachment to the outcome of our actions or those of others. Paradoxically, intimate nonattached human relationships can enjoy a lot more love than conditional intimate relationships.

Detachment leads to isolation, depression, a false sense of separateness, which gets us right back to where we are now. The best alternative may be a 180 degree turn, not a 360 degree spin. Detachment may even give a person a sense he or she is doing great things because the person is aloof, rather than involved. It's just a word, but the power of words is to embody feeling through stated intent.

Non-attachment allows one to be present in the moment. It helps still the mind and calm the heart, as there is no mental chatter about the past or future and no heartstrings strumming a sad song. As my dear friend and author Robyn Bridges so insightfully says, "I know the tremendous stress in the world today, but I choose to embrace the planet and know she loves me back and I feel the joy of that." Awareness of what is and choosing to love and be loved and enjoy, thereby raising our vibrational frequency and amplitude conducts impulses through the etheric medium of the universe, which is one way communication occurs.

Want more connections? Be non-attached. Non-attachment instills shapeshifting connection through presence rather than stagnation and separation through self-importance.

Sacred space is energized by powerful, unconditional, heartfelt thanks. High intensity ayni changes reality. Expect nothing in return, but stay alert. Those connections become more aware of and responsive to us and we to them. Picture every being within your sacred space as non-attached to outcome while actively engaged with you. The idea is not to have random magical, mystical experiences. That's not very useful. The idea is to have ongoing magical, mystical experiences and make them a practical part of life that aids our personal development and joy of being alive. Our joy is a wonderful thing to offer the world; it is ayni at its very best. Staying alert amplifies our awareness of connection. Being in nature and being in the moment offer perhaps the most dependable comprehended feelings of the human spirit, which means having a spiritual and physical experience simultaneously. It's easier than falling off a log – just hug a tree.

It seems foolish and egotistical to think one can improve upon nature before fully understanding her. It seems unwise to interfere with anything we don't understand. The same goes for any intimate relationship and the wisdom behind accepting what is before forcing it to change to become what is not. In other words, one does not necessarily improve a relationship by working to change the other. One improves the relationship by becoming increasingly intimate with the relationship and, most likely, being changed by it. By being non-attached one is able to more fully appreciate what is. Do we want someone to perform surgery on us who has never studied medicine? If not, then why would we accept a relationship with someone who wants to fix us before that person knows us, especially if we haven't asked for the help? When someone does ask for help, though, calling in spirit guides who can help assure the intent and attempted action do not exceed one's ability to help is a good idea.

In relationships of sacred space, we are both host and guest. As a guest, if we remember to leave wherever we are invited better than we found it and, as a host, to serve others, we will not squeeze the life out of the planet or each other as we go about doing something. Everything is always changing and we are here to create changes, not force them. Reality is a dynamic, evolutionary state. Our perception and description of it tend to reflect our state of consciousness, amplified by the wisdom of non-attached actions.

We can change any situation by changing our relationship to it. Once we acknowledge the magical and amusing nature of reality, moments become like a punch line of a good joke because we didn't see it coming. Whenever we answer why? with why not? we are positioned to do something that was impossible just a moment before. So we should understand what we can and get over everything else. That means we don't stand under something that blocks us, we get over it. Non-attachment provides the power for taking a quantum leap. If understanding comes, which it may not, it comes from the larger view of considering larger possibility. The same is true with magic. Reality shifts from "I had an amusing experience," to "I am amusing experience."

Non-attachment acknowledges the playing field will never be level, and also acknowledges the game changes when we see that every person, every thing and every experience has equal value. Without the connection of non-attachment the game is lost, as in this "want of a nail" story.

For want of a nail the shoe was lost;
For want of a shoe the horse was lost;
For want of a horse the battle was lost;
For the failure of battle the kingdom was lost—
All for the want of a nail.
Benjamin Franklin

The implied lesson of the rhyme is that no one foresaw that the lack of such a small thing as a nail would bring down an entire kingdom, although everything in the kingdom was connected. There are approximately nine million species on our planet. Only one species doesn't seem to understand its connection with the others: *Homo sapiens,* maybe because it can't get over its self-importance. We are not just in this together. We are this together. In other words, the nail and the kingdom have equal value.

It's been said we are like gods, so we might as well act like it. The behavior of gods hasn't always been irreproachable, so acting like one may not be the cure-all implied. And ayni is not in the repertoire of most gods. We may be better suited as unlimited beings, rather than gods. It may be better to believe in nothing than to believe in limits. Ayni is a portal into worlds of connectivity, of reciprocity, where words have power, actions have power, experiences have power all designed to increase our awareness of and connection with what is and shapeshift into what can be. Once we allow ourselves access and once access is granted, the rules of the game change because our playing field has become multi-dimensional rather than level.

Traditional lore says there are no inanimate objects. It says there are only animate objects, objects of consciousness because all were created out of consciousness. Rocks are sacred because they are older than us, hence closer to the Creator. Trees are sacred and represent the Three Worlds. Their energy is a lot like ours, when we are at peace. Water is sacred and the first medicine. It sustains life and would not be able to do that if it were not alive. Birds are the embodiment of spirits and air is the breath of the Creator. The list goes on.

To an extent, the power of sacred space depends on how much we trust surrendering to something larger than our ego. Even though everything is connected, our ego can try to dominate or ignore this connection, whether the connection takes the form of the higher self, soul, spirit allies or the Creator. Of course, we can choose how much or how little we try to ignore or dominate this connection. In many ways these choices create our path of possibility within sacred space. Trust requires we let go of where we are and whom we are, in order to be or become something else, acting without knowing the outcome, but trusting we can handle what manifests. That makes living in the magical moment possible. Once compassionate forces of something greater are engaged, there is more amplitude behind ayni, which attracts an even greater compassionate audience, receptive to our offerings.

But don't take my word for it because the truth will not set you free. Only your truth can do that. We can gain insights into our truth through the magic of ayni. Non-attachment is one way to get answers from which to discern our truth.

10

Pace Car or Racecar?

"There is no speed limit on the road of life."
Pagan Youngshadow

After a lifetime of work and raising four kids, all my parents wanted was to stay in their home. It took a lot of work and money for them to stay there and keep the house up, but they managed. They made a few concessions, but as far as getting real in-home help, they did not. My mother took care of almost everything, although more and more was going undone. When my mom's older sister came to visit, there was a bit more to do, and my dear mother had a heart attack.

As my mother staggered, her sister said, "Put your head between your knees."

To which my mom replied, "Josie, I don't think that's going to help this time."

Someone called 9-1-1. My mom actually stood at the door and waited for the ambulance. When she got to the hospital thirty miles away, she flat-lined. [Later I asked her if she saw the tunnel of white light. She laughed and said, "No."]

There was no doubt that once my mom was out of the hospital, she could not return home and care for her husband. In time, they got a nice apartment in a retirement home. But the upheaval was tremendous, leaving the home they'd been in for 50 years.

This happened shortly after the Crash of 2008, so there were few homebuyers, especially in a small Kansas town. Through ceremony, hard work and good fortune – as well as a bit of magic – the house did sell, though, and for a decent price. But a couple of years later, my dad passed and so my mom took another big hit. Still her attitude was remarkable. She reveled in the sixty-four years the two of them had together.

My dad lost his mother when he was seven years old. It made a tough time growing up even tougher. She seemed to be a wonderful woman and radiated peace and beauty from the old time pictures I saw of her. Once as my dad and I sat outside we heard the coo of a mourning dove. He told me he didn't like that sound because he heard it the morning his mother died. I found that interesting and felt obliged to tell him that mourning dove was spelled m-o-u-r-n-i-n-g and not as I thought he thought it was spelled, which was m-o-r-n-i-n-g. He did not believe me. I went in and got a bird book and showed him it was true.

He gave his classic response. "I'll be damn," he said as he looked at the page through his bifocals.

A few hours after my dad's funeral and "after-party," my older sister and I sat outside my parents' retirement home. There was a teeny puddle of rainwater at our feet. A mourning dove fluttered down and landed in the puddle, with water slightly up its skinny little legs. I could have touched it with my foot. It didn't drink; it just stood there sideways to us with its feet in the water. I told my sister about our dad and mourning doves. She hadn't heard that story before. When I was done telling it, the dove flew away.

I am no bird expert, but I do observe them. I've never seen a mourning dove behave that way. It's not like we were at a bird feeder and this bird was used to us. Quite the opposite. Yet, there we were and there it was. Both the timing and the appearance made this experience profound...magical.

What is the best thing to do when such things happen? Like at any magic show, sometimes it's best to enjoy and appreciate, rather than try to understand. What are the odds something like this would happen at that time and place? Slim and none, probably. And that is part of being within a magical universe. I took it to be a tribute to my father and his memory of his mother. But for years I had a nagging feeling about that mourning dove. Unusual animal behavior is often a message, and that bird seemed as if it tried to tell me something more. Nearly five years later it came to me in meditation. It told me my dad had made peace with his memory of mourning doves taking away his mother because, after eighty-seven years without her, he reunited with her in the spirit world as mourning doves fluttered and cooed around them. What a reunion that must have been. As don Oscar says, "Death restores what life takes away."

Sacred reciprocity won't stop personal loss, but it can help us get over loss sooner. When my mother was instantly thankful for their many years together, it made all of us appreciate her, dad, them and what they had received and given all the more. To cry smiling, hurt joyfully, live appreciatively and humbly, joke, drink and toast respectfully and accept that whether one is in the flow or out of the flow is a moment-by-moment choice. The sincerity of going to a loved one's grave to pray and leave offerings is one small way to practice sacred reciprocity. The planet's acknowledgement can come back as quickly and simply as a mourning dove at your feet after a funeral, communicating in a way *that's just for you.* These are messages emblazoned in our memory like an Egyptian hieroglyphic carved in granite. That's the real magic of the moment, that truly personal communication between us and whatever it is that has something for us that it wants us to understand. The timeless quality of such interactions gives us the appreciation we need to be in the moment. Appreciation fuels the fuel we need that gives us the speed to engage with whatever comes our way.

We are built for speed. We have tremendous potential for thought, creativity, vitality and action. People often tell me they feel the assaults on our natural environment, and the pollutants of our built environment, coupled with their increasingly fast lifestyles, make life more stressful. Consequently, it's harder to stay healthy. When I was in grade school, even the Catholic nuns told us that by the time we became adults, we'd be working less and playing more than our parents ever dreamed possible. What happened? How did Sister Bonaventure get it so wrong?

Considering our boundless potential, it seems the problem may not be that life is moving too fast, but that we are moving too slowly to catch up. It may be that our busyness and numbing daily routines actually slow us down because they direct us away from pure pursuits of happiness and potential. Somewhere we may have become convinced it's better to drive with the brake on, while our heart cries out to open up the throttle. If an Indy-500 racecar is driven at 30 MPH for long, soon the once-purring engine begins to sputter because it's built for speed. Confine a magnificent human being in a repetitive routine and most people will look for escape rather than involvement. Without involvement, there is no evolvement.

While the modern world may tend to reduce us to couch potatoes it is imperative we remain spiritually predacious. As routine slows us down, we are put on a diet that's like sustaining ourselves on overly processed food rather than from natural sources. Every step we take away from direct, consciously involved experience adds another middleman to the process, further removing us from the high-octane experiences we innately crave, and further devaluing our experience of life. As we slow down, we clog up. Our emissions become toxic. We spend more time and money in the pits and less on the road. We can adapt to low-octane fuel, such as processed foods and risk avoidance, but it keeps us from running at top speed. After we adapt, low grade fuels are all we want and all we think we can use. By then, we have forgotten our racecar pedigree and that all we need to do to speed up and purr is clean the engine and get back on high octane again.

When on the road of life, it makes no difference whether we see the tank as half empty or half full. What matters is that we keep driving and enjoy involvement with the moment, knowing that whatever filled the tank in the first place will refill it again. The secret of a full tank is balanced fast living, open to the possibility of continual exchange from the universe for our creative, involved actions. So consider two things: use high-octane fuel and keep tuned up to use it efficiently. Healthy expression nourishes this process, as does working together to solve problems to do things better. Expressing the highest good is one of the best ways to give back.

As super-active humans, we live to love, to be and to do. Engaging in life this way, we are responsible for the transformation of the universe and the universe is responsible for us. Metaphorically, low speeds keep us dialed in to the farm report. Exploring self-transformation enables us to pick up speed again. When that engine starts to purr as we approach maximum speed, are we going to be satisfied staying tuned to the farm report? I don't think so. We want to crank up the volume on satellite radio. The road signs of a supportive universe are all around.

We need sunlight and the sun shines daily. We need oxygen and it's everywhere. We need water and it flows. These high-octane fuels are indications of even subtler support systems. When we pollute them, or don't get enough of them, we slow down. Put them to good use. Accelerate first-hand experience. Enjoy high-octane life support. Ride it to the cosmic cornucopia that nourishes human potential. Despite what we've been told, the best way to get excellent mileage and keep our tank full is to step on the gas.

∞∞∞∞∞∞∞∞∞

Body Breathing Practice

To sustain control at high speeds, professional drivers, pilots and athletes find a way to stay calm and at peace. With control at high speed comes confidence and things seem to slow down. The following meditation can develop the inner peace necessary to maintain control and access your inherent speed.

Sit comfortably with back straight. Intend a high degree of general health and peace. Sense the energetic and universal harmony all around you. After a few deep breaths filling the lungs to near capacity, start "body breathing." As you inhale, pull in that energetic harmony through every pore of your skin and take it deeply into your body. Let it pool into your physical center, below your navel. Exhale, intending that everything you receive will be expressed for the highest and greatest good of the planet and all life on the planet. Do this several times. After your body has fully energized, quickly sample the upcoming day, paying attention to situations and people where you may be challenged. Intend to remain fully present and engaged in those times and places. Slow those scenes down to study them, if you want. Remember that life will surprise you with unexpected situations. Recognize them as tests or adventures, not insults. Imagine how to best respond. Try a few different responses to see how they work, then intend to use the most beneficial response, should the situation arise. When complete, take several more deep inhalations and powerful exhalations to reconnect with the harmonious flow around you and to imbue it with your energy. Finish with some stretches of your choice. Yogic sun salutations or the Five

Rites of Rejuvenation[11] are good routines with which to follow this.

Give yourself at least 30 minutes for this meditation, from deep breathing through the stretches. It can be life changing. I can almost guarantee that if you adapt this practice specifically to you and do it frequently, you will develop a practical relationship with the vital energy around you. As your relationship to this energy strengthens, your support accelerates. This relationship dispels routine and super charges the intuition to anticipate and consciously engage the participatory universe in which we live.

I've seen several ways this practice can help in real life. One is that by simply anticipating a good outcome to a challenging situation, let's say a difficult job-related conversation with a boss or co-worker, it can reduce the amount of angst present leading up to the talk. Secondly, anticipating a good outcome is relaxing, thus making more energy available for the actual event, regardless of outcome. This makes a person more effective. The third is one that often happens with this type of mental rehearsal and imagery. That is the desired outcome, or one better, actually occurs. And finally, a quick daily review in the evening can help determine if we can do even better in similar situations the next time.

Here's a true story from a former nurse that demonstrates one way she used a similar technique. Such practices keep us out of the pits.

Night Shift by Nurse Jeri Krenek

I used to work the night shift on a combination rehabilitation & terminal cancer ward. I was one of two charge nurses assisted by two aides. We had a half hour lunch break and two 15-minute breaks per shift. We decided to take our break all at once, for an hour. Two of us would go into the rehab treatment room, lie down on the couches and usually sleep after we ate, while the other nurse and aide covered the floor.

The nurse I worked with most of the time was in her early twenties. The night security guard made a check at least once a shift on our floor. Often while I was on break and the guard came by, he and the nurse would flirt with each other. Because they were so involved with each

[11] Sun Salutations and the Five Rites of Rejuvenation are popular exercise routines that take only a few minutes to get the mind and body right. Descriptions and videos are available online.

other, she would ignore my cancer patients who required frequent pain medication. I could hear them crying out in pain, so I would get up and go take care of them or give them their medication.

I spoke to her about this on more than one occasion but she kept ignoring my patients. Naturally, I was very upset and frustrated. I decided to try and talk to her higher self since I hadn't had any luck with speaking to her directly.

I knew my co-worker's sleep schedule, so one morning I went into meditation and tried to contact her higher self as she was sleeping. I asked her if she would stop ignoring my patients while I was on my break, especially the ones who required pain medication, since she was the only one on the floor who could give it to them.

I didn't work with her for a couple of days after that, but when we did work together again, I noticed I wasn't awakened during my break by people crying out in pain. She was responding to their requests. I couldn't believe it, even though I had made repeated attempts to try and convince her it was the right thing to do.

I was so grateful and happy she had a change of heart and did what needed to be done. I don't know if it was the magic in the contact I tried to make with her higher self or if it was a coincidence. I like to think it was magic.

~~~~~~~~~~~~~~~~~~
~~~~~~~~~~~~~~~~~~

11

Mixed Messages and Paradoxes

"...when the gods want to punish men, first they confused them."
Samael Aun Weor

Paradox is rampant in the world of magic. Danish physicist and Nobel laureate Niels Bohr basically said, "No paradox. No progress." With patience, seeming contradictions and irreconcilable differences begin to give way under the influence of more perceptive living. Keener observation may lead to understanding that we will never understand it all, while opening our world and senses to ever greater mystery and appreciation of it. With luck, such reflection leads to connection and humility. Without luck, it leads to confusion, frustration, feelings of self-importance, and that we've been duped because nothing is at it seems or turns out the way we want. When at such a crossroad, consider that each direction – right, left, back, forward, in, out, up, down, straight ahead or sideways - has its place and time, as well as place in time. Leave an offering at every junction and ask for guidance on which way to go and what to leave behind.

The sacred world is so much more than daily and routine life. Daily life is to the sacred world what the ego is to our total consciousness: a fraction of what is. The sacred world is incapable of sending mixed message because of its primal truth and authenticity, although we can certainly send mixed messages to ourselves and to what is around us. This is not to say people are not part of the sacred world, but most of us perceive some sort of separation between ourselves and almost everything else. Our free will can distort reality.

Paradox is not the same as a mixed message. The sacred world has no agenda other than to be. All it can be is what it is: migrating animals, a tiny seedling growing out of rock, a star, the path of a tornado, the bite of a jaguar, the snap of a dragon, lava flows, daily, nightly and seasonal cycles, the unseen and the dream worlds, all blending into a greater reality of cosmic movement, mystery and creation...what I call *sacrednicity*, the rare phenomenon by which many aspects and entities of the sacred world converge into multiple connections rather than duplicitous actions. It also means to hold many states and actions at once to create sacred space in which sacred reciprocity is offered and received. If we perceive mixed messages in return, what we are getting is either muddled by our interpretation, or something outside the sacred world intends to befuddle us. The sacred world is the ultimate companion, so it will push us into the unknown. There is no better role model of truth, beauty, clarity and understanding than to sensitively perceive how the sacred world receives sacred reciprocity and the outcome of that action. It cannot be what it is not. It will not do what it cannot. It will not expect us to be what we are not. Hamlet was right. To be or not to be is the question. So although Trickster Coyote is always on the prowl, he's being true to his nature, so really, where's the deception? Oh what a web we weave when we allow ourselves to be deceived.

We consciously enter the sacred world to experience and understand non-ordinary realities and explore the limits of our unlimited human potential...another paradox. Communications are clear, albeit often subtle. So we may misinterpret or ignore them. Our attention to the sacred world through ayni hones our understanding of one another. Misunderstanding should lead to greater understanding. During a particular dark Dark Night of the Soul, I asked to understand The Great Mysterious, that all-pervasive source that seems to be the source of all human confusion. I thought I stated it well. However, the universe obliged by giving me more mystery, likely as a way for me to practice unraveling the unfathomable. For quite some time, the more I asked to understand the more muddled things got. I was flabbergasted, considering the intensity of my petitions. After more soulular and cellular buffeting, I finally caught on. 'Ohhhhhh,' I thought. 'The way for me to understand the Great Mysterious is to get more Mysterious, not clarity.' In other words, the Great Mysterious sent me more things I could not understand as I was asking to understand the Great Mysterious, which really can't be done, because once there is clarity there is no mystery. What better way to get an understanding of the Great Mysterious than to experience it to the point where mystery was so prevalent, there was no possible understanding of it? I quit asking that kind of question once I got that kind of answer.

As a way to measure what the planet gives us, economists use the concept of natural capital. The Natural Capital Forum defines natural capital as "the world's stocks of natural assets which include geology, soil, air, water and all living things. It is from this natural capital that humans derive a wide range of services, often called ecosystem services, which make human life possible."

Anyone interested can delve into the concepts of natural capital much more fully. It is acknowledged that nature is priceless, but it does have value. What has not been calculated into this in any way, shape or form is the value of what we do when we give back. Although the above definition claims natural assets include all living things, I have found nothing on the value of what people bring to the table, so to speak. Consequently, we seem to see ourselves both within and without the web of life. This gives me pause. Even the gods don't confuse me this much.

I imagine it is impossible to calculate our contributions and that's probably as it should be. It's like measuring joy and happiness. How do you put value on your first real kiss? Your first fish? Your first dance? Your first born? Like natural capital, such experiences are priceless. The idea is not to measure the benefits, but rather to acknowledge that our connection with all that is has value.

Tangential to natural capital is another term known as Return on Investment – ROI. One popular investment idea is to get as much back as quickly as possible, so we can re-invest and get more back.

Although it's made to be the total truth, ROI is only half the story, if that. What's equally important is our ROE, our Return on Expression. Ideally what we invest in makes us happy – in ways that accommodate the next seven generations is also a nice touch. But as we go and grow through life, there seems to be a tendency to go from playful heart-centered ROE to responsibility-infused ROI, and then back to ROE, if and only if living for ROI hasn't killed, maimed or jaded us as we stumble into retirement. To put it more understandably, we go from living through the heart when we are young, to living through the head when we are adult, then attempt to retrace that seventeen inch or so journey back to the heart later in life, if we are able. The heart is both the center and portal of expression. We can do a lot of stuff, but it may not serve us if we do not authentically serve what we do by authentically serving who we are, even if we do well what does not serve us. The best way to do something is to maximize ROE by doing something from and for the heart. That's being authentic. Medical research even has shown that people who get first heart attacks aren't necessarily the ones engaged in classic risk factors, such as smoking and obesity. According to a report titled *Work in America: Report of a Special Task Force to the Secretary of Health, Education and Welfare,* studies go back as far as 1972 showing that the best predictor of coronary artery disease is low job satisfaction; the second is low overall happiness. This is echoed by a 2011 study published in the July 4 edition of the European Heart Journal.

Too often a professional and family life dedicated to ROI leaves "the investor" bewildered and beleaguered when the time comes for ROE. Minds and bodies are shot. Some people even claim aspects of the health and care system are designed not to keep us healthy, but to take away what we've garnered from a life of ROI. Considering the dilapidated minds and bodies of many of our hardworking seniors, that may have some validity. In any case, authentic expression is a skill. It's not a right or a gift; it's an option. And it's difficult to re-learn it after a lifetime of ROI. So in our later years, many of us carry on with what we've done during our ROI time, and that is try to survive. We behave in order to have, which is usually the core of long term mixed messages. It may be a bit harsh, but even business coach Sandy Gallagher says, "For most people, when their heart stops beating it will be a mere formality."

I lead critical thinking seminars for first year students at Montana State University. I normally start each class period with something we refer to as "*La Question du jour,*" translated as the question of the day. Sometimes students ask the question, sometimes I do. One day I asked,

"Do you prefer to be in love or at peace?" Every single student in two sections replied, "At peace." These are mainly 18 year olds. I find this absolutely astounding they have that much wisdom, considering how inundated we are to be in love, but so little to be at peace. This is the only *question du jour* that's gotten a unanimous answer. (However, at the end of class I tell them they really don't have to choose because they can have both.)

Being at peace, or simply being peace, is a state that creates the space that draws powers and guides to us. When at peace, the mind is quiet, the heart is calm, the body relaxed and resultant right action is focused. It's difficult to send the universe mixed messages when in that state. Sacred space can guide us to our best ROI and ROE by making us more sensitive to what we sense. Coupled with sacred reciprocity, we won't turn our back on our heart.

Is this self-centered? Yes. Is this self-serving? Sure. Is it self-absorbed? Of course, but it also leads to self-knowledge and the confidence and competence necessary to take right action, which is maybe the best and most proven way to give back, and why it is an ayni endorsement and not an Ayn Rand endorsement. Ayni builds a balanced two-way path between the head and the heart, paved with attentive, intuitive, appreciative feeling, thinking and action. These increase the vibration at which we operate and bring more information to us in various ways. Higher thought is not necessarily thinking. Higher thought can be intuitive guidance apart from any conscious desire to direct an answer or outcome. Answers may come immediately or over time, whether awake or dreaming. Be open and attentive. Your body will let you know what feels right, so go with that. Some people use muscle testing or a pendulum for yes or no answers, and that's great. Sacred space and sensitivity can provide much more detail.

Before we go any further, let's discuss this concept of vibration, which gets tossed around a lot in personal growth circles. The state of vibration can be thought of as a quality of energy and, as everything is energy, everything has a vibration. Many people say a higher state of consciousness has a higher vibration. By comparison, mean, depressed people – those with negative emotions and behavior – have a low vibration. Hitler is a favorite example for such comparisons, although not one of mine. In any case, the prevailing thought is that a high vibration is better.

That's just part of the story, too.

Here's another part. Let's say you're in a group of about a dozen people waiting for a meeting to start. Others come in one by one and say their hellos. Of course, each person has a different vibe. The happy, the sullen, the obnoxious – all give a different impression based upon their personality, mood and even station in life, so to speak. The energy of the room shifts whenever someone new comes in and the energy will likely shift again as the meeting starts. Then attention shifts to the speaker and impressions are made according to the speaker's energy.

The point is that we sense the energy around us all the time. But what we really respond to is the amplitude of the energy, which is the power behind the thought. So, a low vibration that we call angry can be extremely toxic to everyone in the room if it has a lot of amplitude behind it, whereas a kind person with no energy has little, if any, impact even though a kind person may be "vibrating" much higher.

I know a few laws of physics. My favorite is F=MA. It means Force equals Mass times Acceleration (speed.) I made up another. I call it the Law of Vibrational Impact and calculate it according to what I call the Impact Equation.

Here it is.

Impact = Attitude(Amplitude^2)/Time

The shorthand is $I = A(A^2)/T$

I put each variable: attitude, amplitude and time, on a scale.

Attitude ranges from "in the toilet," which is zero, to "in heaven," which is a 10.

0 1 2 3 4 5 6 7 8 9 10

Time ranges from the "speed of light =1" to "stands still = 10"

1 2 3 4 5 6 7 8 9 10

Now, here's the kicker: amplitude. Amplitude is the power behind the feeling; emotional content. I square it to counter that misguided Law of Inverse Squares, which does not account for the participatory quantum universe of like attracts like. Besides, a mathematician friend told me if I ever wanted to come up with a credible equation, one variable had to be squared.

Amplitude ranges from "dead," which is zero, to "if I was any better I'd be twins," meaning you are busting out of your mind and body with energy. This is a 10. Amplitude is another way of saying emotional content. It means, "Have heart. Commit. Feel. Act with power, conviction and focus."

0 1 2 3 4 5 6 7 8 9 10

Let's put some numbers into the impact equation and see if it makes sense in the following story.

Ernie did not make his sales quota this month and is livid. His attitude is usually arrogant, unless he wants something from someone, but now depression, anger and self-importance are rampant. Ernie knows his customers don't realize how stupid they are and that enrages him even more. He drank all weekend and showed up for work Monday, intent on making someone pay for his bad luck.

What sort of impact will he have?

Being vindictive is not going to make him many friends, but he's not quite in the toilet. Let's give Ernie a 1 for attitude, a low, almost in the toilet, vibratory state.

However, being vindictive will drive Ernie pretty hard. His intensity is way up there. He could stroke out. Fortunately, he has a semblance of self-control, but overall his energy is unmistakable. He's pissed; no mixed messages. Let's put his amplitude at 9.

He was like this for a few days, so the weekend dragged by for him, knowing he could do nothing for those two days. To him, weekend time was a 6, not quite slow as molasses, but close. He was impatient and felt there was nothing he could do until Monday. He spent a lot of time draining beer bottles and blowing them away with his shotgun. That was a lot of fun. His dog hid from him.

This is how Ernie's weekend measured.

Weekend Impact Score = $1(9^2)/6 = 13.5$ on the Impact Scale. That is, 1 times 81, divided by 6 = 13.5.

However, on Monday, when he was able to do something, the influence of time changed for him, his mood slightly improved because he could put his hostility into action. So, time substantially speeded up for him. These are his Monday numbers.

Monday Impact Score = $2(9^2)/3 = 54$.

If Ernie could improve his attitude with his current intensity, he could really make positive change. However, most doctors would probably concur his stress level and lifestyle aren't healthy, so his health will likely deteriorate. Although Ernie quadrupled his Monday morning impact score compared to the weekend, the attitude that drives it is harmful to him, and likely won't make him a lot of friends or customers.

Ernie's co-worker, Susie, is a soft spoken and gentle person in the front office. She loves people and cats and routine. Always bubbly, her outer attitude is usually high, but on the inside she wishes for more and wants to be loved. This particular Monday her combined attitude is a 5, a modest vibratory rate. Her co-workers like her, but feel she's way too passive. So, let's give Susie's amplitude a 3. Time is like a rainy Sunday afternoon for her, rather dull, but comfortable...if she turns up the thermostat in her apartment.

Susie's Impact Score = $5(3^2)/4 = 11.25$

From these two examples, it can be discerned that although Susie is vibrating at a rate considered to be five, which is 2 1/2 times greater than Ernie, Ernie's amplitude gives him an impact score nearly five times greater than Susie's. Ernie will impact his space and the space of others more than the high vibrating Susie.

Finally, let's look at Sondra. Optimally engaged with self and others, Sondra is a realistic optimist who takes full responsibility for herself. She puts compassion into action through self-care and appreciation for the larger world, and by being a fulfilled and consummate professional. If she needs to make a change, she makes it. So her attitude usually hovers around an 8. Her engaged attitude keeps her amplitude at a consistent 7. Consequently, time goes by fast, which tends to keep her in the flow, as well.

Sondra's Impact Score = $8(7^2)/2 = 8(49)/2 = 196$

Wow! Sondra is going to rock our world!

These scores are arbitrary, but no more so than some other scales people devise. The point is that as we speed up by being present and engaged, time slows down – or changes altogether – as we "do something." Putting a vibrational impact of 196 into our sacred space as opposed to 13.5 will have a dramatic difference on our life experiences. This exercise demonstrates how our impact is a moment-by-moment affair and takes awareness and intent and presence to consistently impact our sacred space and world in ways that help assure we don't send mixed messages into them.

To operate at a higher level, try this 3-part formula. Do something kind for yourself. Do something kind for someone else. Do something kind for the planet. Every day.

~~~~~~~~~~~~~~~~~~~

Energizing Sacred Space Practice

Part I

Sit comfortably and straight and begin deep breathing. Pull the abdomen in to move the diaphragm so your lungs can fill. Visualize a stream of light energy above you. Pull that in through your crown, down your spine and allow it to pool in your lower abdomen as you hold your breath. Exhale and relax. Repeat several times.

Next, still being conscious of your breath and drawing it into your abdomen, hold your breath and imagine a space between your hands just above your lap about the size of a soccer ball. As you exhale, exhale out your hands and your forehead into that space between your hands. Inhale and hold again. Now work your hands back and forth in that space, bringing your hands close together and then apart. Exhale again, out your hands and forehead, increasing the amount of power coming out your hands and forehead.

Breathe in again and hold. Double the space between your hands, working it as you move your hands back and forth. Let your arms be pliable. Exhale again into that space. Pour energy out your hands and forehead into it as if it were coming out of a fire hose. Increase the power. Do this several more times.

Sense the energy between your hands. Discern if you want to keep it or get rid of it. We can't leave energy balls lying around as someone could fall over it, so if you want to keep it, push the energy ball either into your abdomen, heart space, forehead or anywhere that needs energy. If you want to get rid of it, push it into the floor or the ground. If you push it into the floor, know that the energy will follow the foundation of your living space into the ground and dissipate there.

Part 2 - Do this next part with a partner

After making and releasing the energy ball, stand up and face a partner about three feet away from you. Make sure you both have plenty of room to move backwards, at least ten feet or so each. With your hands facing your partner's hands, begin to pour energy out both of your
~~~~~~~~~~~~~~~~~~~

hands and forehead into your partner's hands. Now walk towards each other and get close, but don't touch. Now move back. Now forward. Now back. Now keep backing, as your pour energy out, maintaining the connection.

When ready, separate from your partner. Each of you should put your hands together to hold your energy ball. Determine whether to embody it or let it go and do so. Share any impressions you want.

Make energy balls any time. Share them with family, your sacred space and your sacred objects. Trade them with your friends! Collect all seven and a half billion. They are a wonderful gift.

Part 3 – Do this in your sacred space
Sit and relax while doing several deep abdominal breaths, pulling light energy through your crown, down your spine and allow it to pool in your lower abdomen. With eyes closed, become fully aware of the space around – front, sides, behind, above, below – and within. Sense objects and anything else you want in any direction. Be especially mindful of the areas behind, above and below you.

When ready, fill the space three feet/one meter in every direction with your highest energy, pouring it out every pore, especially your hands, tailbone, feet, heart and forehead. Double it…both space and energy. Keep increasing the space and energy until you are at your maximum. Determine the farthest extent of your awareness and hold that for a while. Notice any other changes in you and your space.

Release all that energy for the highest and greatest good. Take a few conscious breaths as you return to full body awareness. When ready, slowly open your eyes.

Purpose – Most of us are blessed with wonderful eyes and ears. It's a good idea to rest them from time to time and develop our tactile sense and intuition, by becoming more aware of what's going on in spaces around us that we don't see, such as what's behind, above and below us.

∞∞∞∞∞∞∞∞∞∞∞∞∞∞∞∞∞∞∞∞∞∞∞∞∞∞∞∞∞∞∞∞

The Loving Someone You Don't Practice

It's easy to feel love when we think of someone we love. So, think of whom you love the most. Hold the person in your mind's eye and heart. Let absolute and boundless love fill you for him or her.

Now, think of a person for whom you have very strong hostile emotions. Fully experience why you don't love that person. Hold the person in your mind's eye and heart. Then shift your feelings and let absolute and boundless love fill you for that person, re-experiencing the same love you have for someone you really do love. Hold that impression and send that love to him or her. Go back and forth with this. Imagine someone you love, and then transfer those feelings to someone you don't. Practice giving love to the unloved until it's genuine.

When doing this practice, notice what emotions come up. Go deeply into these feelings. Keep going back and forth until you can at least accept, if not love, the person you could not before. Using pictures of each person makes this more powerful. Do your best to re-experience positive feelings toward the "unloved" when that person spontaneously comes into your mind...or the physical space or your daily life. I can almost guarantee if you do this exercise and feel the love, you will change your relationship with people who unsettle you. Through that, you will change your relationship with sacred space, with personal relationships and with the world, especially when you take the sacred space of your heart out into the world. When I do this, I notice I begin to see a bigger picture of why things are as they are. I am less likely to judge or attack, and more likely to let go of negative emotions and act appropriately.

If this practice doesn't work for you, put a picture of the person you don't love on a tree and hug it. That should do it...

12

A Clear Choice

"A coward dies a thousand times before his death, but the valiant taste of death but once."
William Shakespeare – Julius Caesar

When we talk of free will and what it is, it may be that all free will comes down to is a choice between fear and love. Our major decisions and boldest actions are a choice between these two, whether to act out of fear or love. Many minor decisions are, as well. FDR knew exactly what he was talking about when he said, "The only thing we have to fear is fear itself."

Ayni is a planetary, cultural, social, institutional and possibly a universal phenomenon. So, it is not surprising it is an individual one, too. How much should we expect or request institutions or professions to express reciprocity? How much should those who run public and commercial enterprises engage in public reciprocity? Reciprocity extends beyond a thank you, especially to the natural and etheric realms that support us. Ayni can be thought of as both non-denominational and omni-denominational, if that is a concern. A question is, "How can ayni transform our world for the highest and greatest good?"

With that question asked, it can be related to moving from fear to love. Fear often crams belief at non-believers, who are also known as free thinkers, because the dominant culture seems to fear anything outside its comfort zone. Ayni is based on honest appreciation and gratitude. The ceremonial beauty of ayni makes it powerful, but offerings to benevolent spirits, allies, mythical creatures and sacred space, that is to something other than an anthropomorphic god or angels or saints, can make some people uncomfortable, although ayni can be offered to such entities, as well. The point is, it doesn't matter how we move from fear to love as long as we do, but it does takes courage. Nick Polizzi, Director of The Sacred Science agrees. He said, "The currency in this game isn't money, it is courage."

Ayni is not a panacea, a suit of armor, or bargaining chip. It enables us to live more fully and more aware. It's a change of perspective, not an invitation to invite fear or anything else into our state of being. There's more to being alert in life than looking both ways before we cross the street. Awareness helps us take right action. Right action leads to better outcomes. Those outcomes are not reasons why we reciprocate. We reciprocate unconditionally to honor and strengthen our connections with what sustains us in this space and in this reality so we can go on to others. Ayni lightens any burden we carry.

Obviously, living in reciprocated harmony does not protect individuals and cultures from being deprecated by outside forces. Yet, history tends to look at these events from a lens of immediacy, that is, what happened at the time. What intact indigenous cultures are trying to show now, what ancient wisdom is trying to make us aware of now, is that we don't need to intentionally make life harder on anyone. Life is hard enough just by itself. So, let's support each other, quit messing with each other, and know the challenges of physical reality are more than enough to keep us challenged without fabricating new ones based in fear that make life unnecessarily difficult for all of us. Authenticity is the best policy.

Becoming and being authentic is conscious evolution. The sacred world directs us to our higher authentic self because, judging by its authentic behavior, the sacred world is already there. Within the sacred space of sacred reciprocity we resonate with that. When authority directs us to deny and misdirect our feelings and told it's for our own good, how can we convince or assure ourselves that being authentic leads to the higher self? By questioning. When we do what is best for us, we do what's best for everyone. How can this not be so? The challenge is to truly know what is best for us then take the right action to bring it about. We get information and feedback about this moment by moment. We must act upon that moment by moment, with an eye on a tomorrow that considers the welfare of seven generations. This is the developmental challenge and path to greater knowing and all-serving action through a type of visionary tri-location of past, present and future and all things in between, couched in the eternal now.

In an interview Bruce Lee said, "To me, ultimately to me, martial arts mean honestly expressing yourself. Now that is very difficult to do. I mean it is easy for me to put on a show, be cocky, and be flooded with a cocky feeling and then feel like pretty cool and all that. Or, I can make all kinds of phony things blinded by it or I can show you some really fancy movement. But to express oneself honestly, not lying to oneself and to express myself honestly, that, my friend, is very hard to do."

Expressing oneself honestly to others is also very hard to do.

The choice is authority or authenticity. That's another way of saying the choice is between fear and love. What do we have to do to let the higher self and ayni lead to love? First, simply be open to the possibilities. The higher self is that which leads to and connects us with our highest evolutionary purpose and its pursuit for the greatest good, but not necessarily its accomplishment. In this light – and light is what it is – the evolutionary purpose is integrated into our foundation and our foundation is elevated into our highest purpose. The higher self is not separate from any other part of us, of course. Access to it is a choice, the potential of which vibrates into kinetic expression when the intent is given. Or, when we resonate with the higher vibratory states of human experience. It is attained when we give ourselves permission to experience that which may have been denied us by others who once had authority over us. Ayni fosters self-love when we sense we are loved and accepted by that which is connected to us. When we stay in a state of thanks, we stay in a state of grace, which is magic.

13

Disciplined Imagination

"Stories of imagination tend to upset those without one."
Terry Pratchett

Don Oscar stresses that imagination and right action need to be in equilibrium. Few thoughts have been more poignant for me than this. I am beginning to think that everything that happens to us is to stimulate our imagination.

According to brain science, the pineal gland is light sensitive and there are pyramidal cells in the pituitary. Science may not yet have totally confirmed that a purpose of these cellular prisms is to break down the incoming ray of light entering the top of our head into all the colors of the rainbow, which are different qualities of energy, and allow us to use them for health and expression. The science of human physiology also accepts that many other structures in the body have a crystalline structure. So what is the purpose of light sensitive and light conducting physiological structures?

Communication. Fast, clear communication.

Cytoplasm, for example, is a flowing semi-conductor liquid crystal. Jack Schwarz described our bodies as "crystal-operating systems." Judy Satori, internationally known for her work for human transformation adds, "The blood also carries light/energy along with oxygen in the hemoglobin molecules within the red blood cells. The red blood corpuscles are actually crystalline. As the blood … literally becomes like a sacred river of light flowing through the body."

In esoteric terms, the body is designed to take light to fire to light. In somewhat less esoteric terms this means we transform spirit to physical matter and back to spirit. To put it another way, we direct imagination into right action, which spawns more imagination. You may prefer the metaphor of infinite to infant to infinite again. Or the construct of from stars to earth to stars, which is another way of saying as above so below, as below so above. You get the point. When we can't completely live on light, we need denser substances to sustain our bodies.

In any case, it seems light-based communication, upon which much of our technology is based, is alive and well in the brain and other parts of the body that use different qualities of electromagnetic energy so that different types of communication or vibration take place. We are light sensitive, crystal-operating, vibration-emitting unlimited beings living in and with subtle fields of energy, with much of our true power derived from how well we discern stimulation that can impede or enhance our energetic flow and imagination for optimal functioning in the world and beyond.

As are computer crystals, our crystalline-based system is a semiconductor. Like all semiconductors, our system can conduct information under some conditions but not others. It takes a certain type of stimulation and amplitude to override the existing program. It's acknowledged we accept programming easily when we are young; it seems more difficult to reprogram ourselves as we get older. Programming comes from our genetic code, the environment, which includes a possible resonant morphic field[12], our individual experiences and how we interpret them, choices we consciously and unconsciously make, and likely past and future lives, as well as the Akashic records[13]. Thus, we constantly interact with energy on many levels. Acknowledging we co-

---

[12] A theory put forth by biologist Rupert Sheldrake, morphic resonance is a process whereby self-organizing systems inherit a memory from previous similar systems. In its most general formulation, morphic resonance means that the so-called laws of nature are more like habits. It also claims each individual inherits a collective memory from past members of the species, and also contributes to the collective memory, affecting other members of the species in the future.

[13] The Akashic records can be looked upon as a theoretical library of light in a nonphysical realm wherein one can access all information.

create through imagination puts the responsibility of transformation where it belongs – on us. Otherwise, where do we stop taking responsibility for our life and begin to assign that to something or someone else? Where is the line? In the sand? In the brain sand? In the heavens? There isn't one. We are either responsible or we are not. We either have free will or we do not. We are either micro-managed by the cosmos or we are not. So the question is: How can we be totally responsible if we are co-creators? Being a co-creator implies we are in this with someone or something else. Creation is a team sport and there is no "I" in team. There is no "I" in Creator, either, but there is an "i" in creation. Thus, we are co-creators because we are connected to All That Is and totally responsible for our relationship to and actions with that connection. We are responsible for the universe and the universe is responsible for us. Being connected makes us no less responsible. If anything, it does the opposite. In other words, we have free will, not quasi-free will or semi-free will...just free will.

Where does thought fit into this? Where does ayni? Ayni stimulates the imagination, which tends to become less imaginative for some as we get older. Certainly genetics seem to become more fixed as we age, and our interactions with life can take a toll. Both of these can reduce our imagination. No one may be inherently and intentionally recalcitrant. It may be that the aging structures of the mind and body need a greater amplitude than the old programming to replace it, especially when the old program is habitual. Simply because the morphic field changes does not mean it has the amplitude to override the information and rutted habits of us who were initially imprinted by an earlier morphic field.

Ayni stimulates awareness through adaptive, rather than repetitive, ritual. Ayni can mitigate stagnation, and maybe aging, because it can focus on the shapeshifting responses of our acts by the seen and unseen world. In other words, when we look for change and intend change, it is easier for us to flow with the flow.

It may be up to us to ultimately determine which of these influences has the greater impact. Knowing the variety of influences impacting us can help us make more aware choices. This may mean we better understand why we do what we do and the impact we can have, as well. This is a power of imaginative thought coupled with right action. This is why I call what is often referred to as the Creator/Creatrix the Imaginator/Imaginatrix.

Sacred reciprocity shapeshifts imagination into disciplined imagination. Imagination is a means by which to expand our worldview, which can sit solidly and creatively on our foundation. There are times unbridled imagination is appropriate, a time to let imagination run wild. Who's to say when a person crosses the line of unbridled imagination to something so chaotic that it can drive a person away from his foundation, that base of stability and sanity, into one or more of many forms of madness from whence the odds of return seem small? Not me. Unbridled imagination has a valid purpose, provided it can be reined in and put into right action, when necessary.

In one of his more famous quotes, Einstein called imagination more important than knowledge. Yet we seem to have a love-hate relationship with imagination, as we go back and forth between an encouraging "Use your imagination," to a derisive, "It's all in your head." Imagination may be more important than knowledge because knowledge tends to limit imagination, whereas imagination expands knowledge. Yet, knowledge provides a framework for imagination, a realm of possibility that expands with experience, leading to wisdom. Ultimately, the limit to imagination is our own imagination and the courage with which we use it. Disciplined imagination serves best when it supports our needs and purpose.

Albert realized man cannot live by knowledge alone. Here is his full quote. "I am enough of an artist to draw freely upon my imagination. Imagination is more important than knowledge. For knowledge is limited to all we now know and understand, while imagination embraces the entire world, and all there ever will be to know and understand."

Whether our internal compass points to fear or love, disciplined imagination drives our direction in life. Imagination complements our free will. It stokes and directs where our actions fall on our comfort zone continuum, which means where we act between the endpoints of fear and love. The paradox is we love our comfort zone and may be afraid to move outside of it…so in this case love limits us. Paradoxically, by experiencing what we fear, we can expand what we love.

Chumming the Cosmos Practice

Chumming is defined as dumping bait or other attractant into the water. It is something people do to bring fish to them. Illegal in many places because it leads to overfishing, we can nevertheless use a similar technique to get the attention of benevolent allies when in sacred space. What I call Chumming the Cosmos is simply and respectfully calling the spirits in. The technique presented here has a multi-dimensional twist to it. We aren't overfishing the cosmos. We are simply making potential allies aware of our presence.

To begin, imbue your sacred space with sound from the three-dimensional world, such as song, chant, rattle, bell, flute, drum. Energize your sacred space with positive emotions, such as love, appreciation and peace. Burn incense or smudge with whatever pleases you. Relax. Get comfy.

When passion, incense and sound are brought from the 3D world into an imagined one, we override the law of inverse squares because we put energy into the infinite from beyond our physical body. So picture an appealing scene outside and away from you, but don't go there. Stay within your 3D space, as you watch the scene in front of you. The scene can be a physical place you know and love or somewhere you have never been, either in this dimension or another, in this time or another. It can be among the stars, in the ocean, or to whatever draws you. From your current vantage point, drum or rattle into that scene and observe how the sounds made here impact what is there. This is the cosmic chumming. If the scene fades, energize it with light from your brow. Through this you can experience for yourself whether or not your sounds extend their impact over great distances and into new dimensions and realities. It's that simple. In time, entities from those dimensions may follow that sound into your sacred space to assist in ayni. So keep a good intent as you do what you do. In the unlikely event anything approaches with which you feel uncomfortable, forcefully command it to go back. And it has to. The invitational power is yours and yours alone.

Benevolent allies are always available to help, too. Respectfully, reverently find them and invite them. The journey may be two-way. They may invite you to their place. You can always have a trusted other drum for you who can call you back, if necessary. Your assistant should send the allies back to their realm, as well. This way, nothing gets lost or stuck. We are interdimensional beings and we naturally do this in our dreaming. This practice helps one extend one's self beyond the ordinary in a more conscious way.

It's also important to keep in mind that not everyone visualizes to the same degree. Some people perceive with senses other than vision. It might be sound or feeling or smell. It's all valid. Practice helps.

Doing comparable exercises with others can help repair areas or people damaged by exploitation or change a nasty situation. There is plenty of evidence of how focused communal intent works. For example, in 1988 there were tremendous fires in Yellowstone National Park and surrounding areas. One community near Gardiner, Montana was encouraged to pray to stop one fast moving fire when their homes were threatened. This was a community of the Church Universal and Triumphant, a religious group that did not enjoy a lot of local support at the time. In any case, people from the church prayed for the fire to stop. For some reason, they were ridiculed when there was no spiritual intervention, but rather it was the U.S. Forest Service that stopped the fire at the church's property boundary by aerial spraying of fire retardant. Yet, this seems to be prayer in action. As Pope Francis said, "First you pray for the hungry. Then you feed them. This is how prayer works." In its own way, this was a sacred fire. It was cleaning a lot of natural debris. It just didn't need to take homes out to do its job. Right action is a win-win.

∞∞∞∞∞∞∞∞∞∞∞∞∞∞∞∞∞∞∞∞∞∞∞∞

14

The Imagination – Intuition Conundrum

"In science, the obvious role of imagination is in the context of discovery. Unimaginative scientists don't produce radically new ideas."
The New York Times

"In life, the obvious role of imagination is in the realm of creation. Unimaginative people don't produce radically new anything."
Pagan Youngshadow

For now, let's consider imagination to be more than daydream escapes or the low amplitude monologue of the internal dialogue. The something more is disciplined imagination. Disciplined imagination is a way out of what isn't real.

Discipline is not control. It is intent. It is focus. Disciplined imagination is key to personal heartfelt expression and freedom. Focused intent keeps imagination from becoming a swirling, unruly, chaotic, confused mess. Focused intent releases disciplined imagination. It empowers the mind, brain, heart, body and soul to take the right action necessary for the soul's highest expression of creation. This enhances our mutual relationship and responsibility.

What's interesting in terms of our place in the universe is how this, too, falls on a spectrum of importance on how we view ourselves. On one hand, there are people such as extraterrestrial contactee Enrique

Villanueva, who shares what it's like to be face to face with multidimensional beings of unconditional love and reaching the next level of human consciousness. Enrique says, "We are not only alone in the universe. We are not this tiny little speck in the middle of the universe. We are so huge. So big. We are the whole universe, compressed somehow, in this tiny particle [that] we are."

On the other hand, galactic astronomer Dr. Brent Tully says that there is so much going on beyond ourselves in the universe that it can make us feel very unimportant to the universe. Tully adds, "Humanity must be inconsequential in the grand scheme. The 10 millennia of human existence is just one millionth the history of the universe. There are probably a billion planets in our galaxy with some form of life. There are presently billions of galaxies within our horizon and who knows how many beyond. Then plausibly there has been an infinity of universes present and past. These facts won't deflate some, but some of us might feel humble."

How do these two views impact our actions: the idea we are the whole universe or that we are inconsequential? What should we believe? Maybe we are the whole universe, as Villanueva claims, and we are inconsequential within the realm of infinity universes, past and present, as Tully observes. (Maybe the universe, itself, is inconsequential.) Either perspective inspires awe and, I feel, a reason to not hold back. We have nothing to lose being who we are, doing something we need to do. But what they and others agree upon is that we do come from the stars. Of that, there is no doubt.

Thus, from the divine human perspective, disciplined imagination helps create reality, solve problems and improve life. Let's say that by definition, disciplined imagination includes action. Whether or not disciplined imagination creates the cosmos or the other way around, I don't know. In any case, it seems logical that what exists within us also exists within the cosmos...and the other way around. It seems imagination must come before intent and before creation. Without imagination the Void remains the Void, if it exists at all. Whether subjectively or objectively, at the very least disciplined imagination is a prime player in a creative cosmos. Imagination gives creation a more playful context than creation has by itself. Without imagination, we probably would live in Newton's mechanistic universe. However, quantum physics states that is not true; we live in a probability universe. I have to say that imagination is the heart of reality and the pulse of the universe. Disciplined imagination directs the imagination with a specific intent toward manifestation of that intent and to the greater awareness and connections that ayni creates.

Disciplined imagination is a perceptualizing and initiating force through which all comes into being. Imagination, considered the purview of writers and artists, inventors and scientists, comes from the highest realms of creation; hence we all have it. Many cultures refer to their Top God in some way as Creator/Creatrix, but rather than espousing divinity as Creator/Creatrix, God/Goddess or Father/Mother, the term Imaginator/Imaginatrix implies the male and female components of creative and disciplined imagination as a primal creative influence. Our senses and our imagination impact one another.

Our unconscious exchange of human disciplined imagination with the disciplined imagination of more subtle realms is always present. Ayni develops and maintains a conscious exchange of disciplined imagination because it keeps us present and open to how our ayni is accepted. Ayni sensitizes us to sensing how our offerings are received. Sooner or later, we sense the world responding to our requests. This conscious flow *is* the magic of imagination. "Sacred Fire. Won't hurt anything," is a statement of fact and trust, as well as an appropriately answered prayer because of Wallace's focused intent in sync with the flow of giving and receiving. Wallace was not only speaking as Wallace, but also as an emissary of the Imaginator/Imaginatrix. They were one. The sacred connection was established. When we speak of all being connected, this is an example of what we mean. Ayni stimulates the highest possibilities of disciplined imagination and creative, fun, intelligent, intuitive and appropriate reciprocity. It's a two-way street that gets stronger with use because, paradoxically, it keeps us out of the rut of routine or thinking we know it all. Ideally, the immensity keeps us humble; the potential keeps us inspired.

Without Wallace's action-prayer, the world would still be perfect. It would not have rained, there would have been no sweat, but the world would be as it should be. With his action-prayer, it rained, there was a sweat and the world was as it should be, because the world is a product of the intent of disciplined imagination. Imagine something different, the world is still perfect, but different. The difference is the intent for the highest and greatest good. Without disciplined imagination rooted in such intent, the world is still perfect, but not at its greatest.

Did Wallace make it rain? I don't know. He certainly trusted that the sacred fire wouldn't hurt anything. With that trust and absolute knowingness, plus his seen and unseen shamanic connections, who knows what forces he put into motion? Words may speak louder than actions. Wallace seeded the clouds with intent. Why is that assumed to be less effective than seeding the clouds with silver iodide?

One of the first times the concept of prayer really impressed me was during a Catholic mass. Kansas was in a drought, which seldom happened in eastern Kansas, known for thunderstorms and tornadoes. Father Walter was at the pulpit and prayed for rain. It was the first time I heard such a public prayer with a tangible intent. Rain. Rain to help the farmers...and not just Catholic farmers. As a little kid, I was in awe, impressed. I thought here was a test not just of faith, but of a priest putting his reputation on the line...on the altar, actually.

Ultimately, it did rain. Where was the thank you? Where was the public affirmation of divine intervention and benediction? The point of the story is not to question the value of prayer. I've brought up its importance earlier. The point is that we tend to undervalue our intent and the manifestation of intent. Saying thank you for making something happen can be wrongly perceived as making something happen. But that's the point. That's the intent. That's the magic. What's the problem? Christ purportedly said, "Greater things than me shall you do" (John 14:12). Accepting the mantle of co-creation is what enables us to move forward. Are we so afraid to acknowledge that intent made it rain so we may have violated someone's water rights therefore ayni is not given because we don't want to be held liable?

When I served mass as a boy, I studied the different techniques and energies the priests brought to the mass. The mass seldom held surprises. Some priests seemed bored; others imposed upon. The really good ones brought power and energy, such as Father Luke. He never seemed to tire of the shapeshifting mystery and creation of the consecration. With body language and powerful incantations, he conveyed the impression he believed in what was happening. I'd ring the bell in support. But during other priests' lackadaisical sermons, I remember thinking, "Good god. If I had a captive audience like this, I'd bring it!" Few priests took advantage of making the Word Flesh...that is, to create, to bring light to fire to light to the faithful. And not one offered a Q & A session during the time set aside for a sermon. What a waste.

When the word is made flesh, it moves us. This happens with sacred reciprocity. That's how we know it's working its magic. When I offer ayni, I imagine I have a captive audience. Waiting. Listening. Wondering. Watching. Wanting to receive. Wanting me to wow them. Praying for my success to wow them. True support. I ring a bell or shake a rattle or beat a drum to bring it.

Imagination opens possibilities of creation. We call what we see by generic names: robin, tree, rock, butterfly, cloud, worm. To get beyond that, I introduce myself when I offer ayni so I am not only known as a two-legged. Otherwise, some aspect of creation might say, "Here comes that two-legged again who burns sage." Use whatever name you know yourself by. It could be your given name, a ceremonial name, a spiritual name, a dream name, a *nom de plume.* Things wish to know you by that which you are known. Natural presences are very respectful and polite. Introduce yourself, and the creations and creatures of nature will introduce themselves to you. Ayni is more affectionately reciprocated among friends than acquaintances. As a matter of fact, I received the name Pagan Youngshadow as I hiked out of the mountains one day and decided to keep it.

When at your altar or nature's altar, imagine what it is like to have a captive audience giving complete undivided attention and being totally present in the moment for and with you. This is nature. This is what's listening and feeling. This is what waits for us and welcomes us. Be so godly and humanly passionate that you hear the plants and animals and spirits say "Alleluia!" when you speak. This is powerful medicine. This is true communicative reciprocity. When done, pause and feel, and offer another thank you. I guarantee that everything that heard you will talk about you when you're gone. Mutual passion and understanding ~ what gifts.

Over the years, I was too stupid to realize how shapeshifting words and sounds could be because I did not understand the importance of putting high-amplitude and honest intent behind them. I was completely fooled, believing actions speak louder than words, when the evidence clearly shows sound-originated mystery is around me. According to the most primal creation stories, word through vibration incites action, thereby making action dependent upon, if not subservient to, speech. We are taught the pen is mightier than the sword, but the spoken word is much more powerful. Word and action are the dynamic duo of manifestation. Thought, word and action are the holy trinity. Thought, word, action and passion are the four horsemen of creation. Thought, word, action, passion and intent are the all-stars of court and cosmos. Consequently, I reviewed some of my actions. Why don't they speak louder than words? Because they don't have the passion and intent behind them that words of passion and intent have.

So, do actions speak louder than words? The answer may be, "It depends..." It may well be that words speak louder than actions, or at least just as loudly and are capable of changing our crystalline structure in ways actions cannot. The Tibetans have a proverb: "There is nothing so feeble as action without prayer." Prayer without action isn't so great either.

Appreciate how ayni is received. Reciprocate without expectation. Act for the highest and greatest good without expecting reward. Foster a mindset and heartset of surrender while taking responsibility. These open magical possibilities of sacred connection, thus assuring the all-important creative connection with the Imaginator/Imaginatrix energies. Disciplined imagination is a link to the divine, the human, the present and the infinite. Considering what we get in return, why would anyone want off magic's magical path? The planet is either magical or it is not. So we either engage with it or we do not. If the planet isn't magical, then neither is life. That makes no sense to me and I wonder how that could be possible.

One challenge with "bringing it" is that although there may be a series of levels of conscious attainment through reciprocity, as well as quantum leaps in understanding, there really is not a series of steps. In other words, a lot needs to be done and come together at the same time. The understanding, actions and intent behind what is done become more refined with practice, patience and persistence. I will offer suggestions, but suggest you yield to your intuition.

Disciplined imagination brings the enviable *Aha! moment,* the epiphany, the realization that drives new action, the insight from which a new branch of thought grows on the tree of conscious evolution. The most profound thoughts and images imaginable have little staying power without the action of experience. Knowledge, through experience with reflection, becomes wisdom. Right action is best discerned through the heart and heart-felt intuition of the disciplined imagination. Right action depends on us having the awareness and courage to acknowledge what we feel. Through that we learn and sense best the way to perform authentic reciprocity without routine steps that don't mean anything. Disciplined imagination helps us think outside our environment…as well as into our environment. It's an ally. As the Captain Morgan rum banner advocates: "Make your legendary ideas a reality!" I'll drink to that.

As we sail our disciplined imagination into the uncharted waters of creation, chances are we will get blown off course. We may wind up someplace we did not imagine or someplace unimaginable. Hence, the need to be non-attached to the manifested outcome, yet self-directed, unimportant, aware and opportunistic. Man was a sailor long before he rode a horse. The best sailors and explorers can handle where they are, even if they don't know where they are, whether in or out of port. Good mariners are always welcome. They have stories, presence, joy and riches. In other words, they have something to offer.

Disciplined imagination directs the action with a specific intent and strategy toward a specific outcome. But even with a strategy and a focused intent, we have to live with the possibility that our plans won't quite go the way we intend and we just might wind up someplace unexpected. Still, there is a lot under our control. We need to learn to work with what we can control and accept what we cannot. Sailors harness the wind; they don't own it and they don't rule it.

Imagination directs us to better observe how the world responds to us for our ayni. In other words, the world always gives us gifts in exchange for ours, but we don't always recognize them. That must frustrate the cosmos to no end. Reciprocity is as much cyclic as it is magic. I know how I feel when I give something really nice to someone, but it's never used. Nice gifts enhance a relationship and when properly used they make things better. Using imagination in ways that allow us to expand awareness is a way to give ayni, so it is nothing to fear and has nothing to fear. We can be so afraid of losing our rationality that we don't use our imagination enough to key upon possibilities we've been offered.

Imagination can be developed and used whether we are asleep or awake. To become more astute handling waking imagination makes one more adept at handling dreaming imagination. In other words, states of dreaming and wakefulness tend to blend into each other after awhile, which is no surprise as this is simply integrating states of awareness into a congruent whole. It does not mean we cannot tell the difference between the two, or that we are fragmented or schizophrenic. Instead, we are more activated, integrated and expanded. Disciplined imagination opens us up to more realms of reality. Most importantly, it enables us to keep the power of creation active and conscious. We are always creating. We tend to be happy when we consciously create because we get excited seeing our heart's purpose and desires alive in the world. When we unconsciously create, we often get a life we say we don't want. We send mixed messages to the cosmos, maybe because we are not taking full responsibility for our life. Life force is dissipated rather than focused. It's pretty hard to be grateful when we live like that. Disciplined imagination helps us reciprocate to the sacred world in the way it gives to us, with no mixed messages and no strings attached. Once we cut the strings and let go, we meld into a flow where nothing holds us. It carries us. Letting go releases an astounding amount of energy.

The sacred world must have an inherent trust of humankind, sensing its reciprocity to us in no way endangers it. This does not seem to be the reality, though, as what we do as people certainly seems to threaten the natural and sacred world. However, disciplined imagination brings about an orderly expansion of consciousness, emulating the orderly expansion of the universe.

For over one hundred years, astrophysicists calculated that the universe was still expanding from the so-called Big Bang, but that in time, the universe would lose its original momentum and start to shrink until it collapsed on itself through the force of gravity. However, recent discoveries from the Hubble telescope and quantum physics show a different story. The universe is still expanding, but now scientists calculate that it's expanding at an ever-increasing rate. The idea is that as the universe expands, gravity has less of an influence on pulling it back together and that's why it's expanding faster. It has also been hypothesized another force is at work in the universe that hasn't been discovered yet. It is called dark energy. What's interesting though is that as the universe expands, it seems to fill with dark energy. Unlike gravity, dark energy does not become weaker with expansion. New dark energy fills the new space of an expanding universe.[14]

We bring additional power to the planet through imagination, activities and creativities. This is why sacred space can become so powerful; we bring extra power into it. Through disciplined imagination and sacred space, our connectivity with the world changes. They are catalysts that make exponential quantum change possible. The synergistic and compatible intent of our allies increases the power of sacred space even more, as we co-create together.

Einstein was likely right imagining that imagination is greater than knowledge, but how far will imagination take us? Modern quantum physics strongly suggests existence is a game of chance that plays by evolving rules based on the observer and likely the number of people agreeing upon what is observed. This is what physicists mean by claiming we live in a participatory universe. As probability decreases, potential increases. It is also well established the brain cannot differentiate between what is imagined by the mind and what is "real." Whether real or imaginary, sensorial impulses are received by the body the same way. How much more evidence do we need that disciplined imagination coupled with right action is perhaps the greatest creative force in the universe? In the quantum vernacular it could be said that what we imagine does not exist and what we imagine does not not exist.

Anyone can safely access the dream world. There are countless stories of dreams manifesting imaginative and right answers to difficult situations. You likely have some yourself. However, opening the channels consciously and building their foundation is paramount to a continuous flow of magic. How do we do that?

Through unbridled use of imagination. Imagination has the same root in it as magic: magi, which is wise. When performing ayni, allow unbridled, disciplined imagination to witness all the ways the world favorably responds. Unbridled. Disciplined. Let it run wild. Turn up your senses, too. Imaginatively consider new possibilities of what's going on. If a bird alights on a branch after you burn sage, for example, acknowledge that. If a breeze softly rustles the leaves and grass after you say thank you with an offering to the water, notice it. If you sense the

[14] One exception to the expanding universe is a gravitational anomaly known as the Great Attractor, an area of space drawing in thousands of galaxies, including our own. The Earth and the Milky Way Galaxy are moving towards it at over 1,000,000 mph/2.200,000km/hour.

unseen spirit world, or an actual, spiritual manifestation, say hello. You may smell incense or something else that seems out of place, to let you know you have a visitor. If thunder cracks to acknowledge a prayer, you've been heard. Say thank you. Welcome and acknowledge these incursions into your physical and spiritual senses. Subtle affirmations happen quickly. It is as if the spirit world tests the waters of our soul to see if we are truly who we say we are. We don't just chum the cosmos. The cosmos chums us.

The sacred world reveals secrets and possibilities to us through signs. Not every portent is a disaster about to happen, thank god, although doomsday prophecies don't sound like a lot of fun. We get them so we can take actions to mitigate them. And, as quantum physics supports the idea that events that occur depend upon what we focus, it might be best to understand it is possible for conscious evolution to occur without the Apocalypse, despite the fact that others seem hell bent on bringing it. The modern world does not help, with all the mixed messages it sends us 24/7 such as, "The sky is falling, but you won't care in a brand new car!"

So, what can be done so ayni helps with the best and mitigates the worst of the prophecies – even our worst self-fulfilling prophecies? What can we do to assure we make the best of the Next Coming of Whatever/Whomever it is that may be returning? Sometimes conscious evolution is as simple as asking the right question. For example, avoid asking, "What is wrong with me?" The universe will answer in what might be painful ways and displays just to show you. Instead ask, "What is the best action I can take now?" Sense the vibration of your question and what you are putting out as you ask. Then patiently feel, observe and intuit what comes back. Relax. It may take awhile, but answers do come.

Despite our propensity for putting our existence on the lip of the abyss of multi-cataclysmic extinction, conscious evolution without doom is possible. On the other hand, we cannot cavalierly assume the universe likes us enough to spin into existence our every intent. If the universe is not a micro-manager, which it is not, then we may not want to be macro-managers and expect to have everything under our control. Yet we have to do something. The best something may be founded in the flow and possibility of disciplined imagination, rooted in our inherent responsibility as co-creators who are sort of 100% responsible for whatever shows up in our life. That is, we are 100% responsible for how we *respond* to whatever shows up in our life, not for everything that is there. We would have to live in complete isolation to be responsible for everything that shows up in our life and we don't. But one thing is certain: the universe won't turn its back on us if we don't turn our back on our heart. When we follow the heart, there is no limit to what we can learn, experience, enjoy and become. Within the expression of purpose, there is no limit. As Ellen Johnson Sirleaf said, "If your dreams don't scare you, they aren't big enough!"

When and how do we let disciplined imagination come out of the closet? How much imagination will we accept? How much deviation from the mean will we accommodate? Should imagination tie in to our foundation? When does the foundation need to be rebuilt? Obviously, when it can no longer support that which it needs to support. Very few people will reduce the weight of their home so that a weakened foundation lasts longer. Neither should we belittle our experiences and possibilities to avoid the painstaking work of building a new personal foundation that better serves our evolving state, which comes about when we question deeply and behave authentically. The Dark Night of the Soul is really a re-construction project.

This brings us to the imagination-intuition connection. The Merriam-Webster dictionary defines intuition as: a natural ability or power that makes it possible to know something without any proof or evidence: a feeling that guides a person to act a certain way without fully understanding why: something that is known or understood without proof or evidence.

Jack Schwarz believed intuition is "When you know, but you don't know how you know." With that as a start, let's explore the imagination of possibility in consort with intuition. We can imagine something we want to do and intuit if it's the right thing for us and, if it is, intuit how to do it. Together imagination and intuition are a net cast out into the waters of possibility and right action.

Imagination and intuition exist outside any confine of time and space...but likely originate from the same place. Feeling, intuiting into these definitions suggests that intuition is based upon a greater awareness of subtlety. According to psychic research, among the most common evidence of intuition is when we sense the phone is about to ring and we know who it is before we answer or look at caller ID. Another common indication is our sensitivity to knowing when someone is looking at us, and we turn to see a pair of eyes looking into ours. After all, everything is always watching. When we grace the natural world with appreciation, we shouldn't be surprised to see a pair of eyes looking at us.

Or one eye. Early one morning after a night along Montana's Madison River, I set up my spotting scope. As I looked through the lens and focused, I laughed. A golden eagle was in a cottonwood on the other side of the river. The trunk hid half of her head, but I could see that single golden eye as she see peered right at me through my spotting scope to check out what I was doing. The thing is, I knew she was there before I saw her. That's how intuition often works. It can be a flash of insight or knowing that happens so fast our logical, rational thinking does not have time to interfere with it. We often act upon it without realizing we intuited right action. Once I felt the intensity of the eagle's gaze, it was hard to imagine ever not knowing she was there. And why would I?

Here's a more practical example of intuition, although I should have known better.

A Flatlander's Vacation

I drove about 1,000 miles one day in my 1970 VW bug, heading to the Grand Canyon from Hays, Kansas for the first time in my life. I don't think I planned on driving that far, but kept pushing until I got into the park. I arrived at night. There was no moon. I parked in a lot, and grabbed my sleeping bag and flashlight. I was so excited I left the tequila in the car. I scooted over a retaining wall, enamored by the stars above me and the desert around me. I was in heaven. I ambled and meandered and then, for some reason, stopped, turned on my flashlight and shined it down between my feet. There was nothing there. I had foolishly walked to the edge of the Grand Canyon. My toes hung over it.

I know I'm not the sharpest knife in the drawer, but something should have triggered something in me when I scooted over the retaining wall, but nothing did. I have no idea what I was thinking. Probably what saved me is that I wasn't thinking. I backed up at least fifty feet before I laid out my sleeping bag, so I didn't roll into the abyss by mistake. I walked to the area at sunrise and looked down. There was no coming back had I gone in. Once I felt the intensity of the Grand Canyon, it was hard to imagine ever not knowing it was there.

~~~~~~~~~~~~~~~~~~~~

Intuition has emotional content. When intuition kicks in, pay attention to it as much as possible, without judging. Many people experienced with intuition suggest we go with the first impulse, like the first answer thought to be correct on a multiple-choice test. As soon as the rational mind kicks in, intuition fades, analogous to waking up from a dream we remember, only to watch it dissolve irretrievably through the mind like sand through a sinkhole.

The marriage of imagination and intuition is capable of producing powerful and magical offspring, greater than the sum of their parents. Intuition can supply the how of how to and the what of what to do next when imagination inspires wondering. When intuition gifts us with right action, ayni should follow.

One February, I wanted a few fresh organic lemons. I went to the food co-op's produce section to get some, but there were none. I wasn't surprised, as I did not know if the co-op had a source for organic lemons during the winter. So, I went to the juice aisle, imagining there would be organic lemon juice. There was. I got a bottle, put it back, and strolled back over to the produce section. The produce manager had just begun to unpack a box of plump organic lemons.

Was this magic? Synchronicity? Coincidence? Am I psychic? Was I privy to the store's lemon shipments? There are other possibilities.

I choose to choose magic. Nascent magic is like puppy love. When just learning the ways of magic, magic can be quite gentle and trusting, coming to us as a puppy squirming on the ground, wagging its tail, hoping for some luvin'. If we love that puppy in return, it becomes more trusting. It begins to approach us more confidently and may even become a protector. But if we mistreat or ignore it, it will either quit coming to us or it will turn against us when it's older. Magic seems to have free will, too. It has volition.

As is imagination, intuition is an aspect of spiritual wisdom. Acting upon it righteously unites us with the moment. When we sense into intuition, right action is immediately and spontaneously imagined and taken. Intuition, imagination and right action are another holy trinity strengthened by use and reciprocity. So, one way I can reciprocate for
~~~~~~~~~~~~~~~~~~~~

getting lemons out of season is to use that experience to tell a story of intuition in a way that inspires others to use theirs.

Spiritual power was and is a part of culture. When showered by such gifts of power, respect, humility and reciprocity traditionally ensued. Sometimes reciprocity included conquest and human sacrifice, although I will assume today's reader is not moved to such action. When we embrace our indigenous nature, we lose the arrogance associated with acting as if we know everything, or that there is no mystery. It is difficult to say which of these attitudes we are better off without.

When we free ourself enough to imagine and open our mind and heart to see to the core of whatever presents itself to us, we may come to see with mythopoetic, kaleidoscopic eyes and nothing will ever look quite the same. It may be that everything that is good for us is unlimited and unconditional ~ magic, love, imagination, intuition, abundance, wisdom, experience. As sacred reciprocity enhances disciplined imagination by activating new possibilities of sensorial, psychic and intuitive connection to our surroundings, disciplined imagination yields unlimited ways by which to show appreciation to all that supports us, ultimately manifested in how we express our heart's true purpose.

I feel obliged to mention the use of psychotropic medicine plants and fungi now, although the topic falls outside of the focus of this book. Using such allies can certainly make one question what is real and what is imagined. However, they well may be one and the same: what is real is imagined and what is imagined is real. More importantly, power plants and mushrooms can open one up to greater possibility and revelatory knowledge, the nature of which often depends upon intent and guidance from one's teacher. Any true seeker approaches power with respect and humility and, in a perfect world, with guidance from a good teacher. If medicines are ingested without proper respect and intent, then, if we are fortunate, their powers hide from us. If we are unfortunate, we may never come back from where they take us, at least not totally. Unless one gets a clear message that undermining health and frying the brain is what one needs for the soul's evolution, I suggest avoiding the reckless use of sacred medicines.

15

Surrender and Letting Go

"If I had asked people what they wanted, they would have said faster horses."
Henry Ford

Everything shapeshifts. Our personal journey is unique and evolutionary while, paradoxically, being part of the collective return to Source. To be in transformation is the natural order of things, an existential paradox. Life can be unnerving when the whole universe is hell bent on change. No one is born to maintain the status quo. We are here to make changes. How can our personal sacred space accommodate universal, world and personal change, while supporting our foundation?

The idea of surrendering to anything, let alone a higher power, baffled me for years. I wasn't the kind of guy to let go and let god. I had to do something; surrender wasn't on the list. As I began to understand we live in a co-creative universe I began to understand surrender. Nothing of value happens without taking chances; surrender is no different. It takes courage. This kind of courage means to let go of what does not serve us and of what keeps us from being who and what we are meant to be.

Sacred space evolves according to how much we trust surrendering to something more powerful and graceful than our ego self. Even though we are all connected, the ego or personal self can choose to ignore this connection, whether it's called the Higher Self, Soul, God, Source, Great Mystery, Web of Life, whatever. Sometimes we ignore this a little; sometimes a lot. I ignored it a lot. Surrender also means to let go of egocentric isolation and what we ignore in order to connect with and embrace more of what is, by whatever name we call it. In other words, let go of smallness, surrender to largeness to receive the largesse of the universe within sacred space. Surrender is the only way to stop giving power away. It's no paradox because being you is possible only through a higher power, which is also you. I think this is convolutedly cool.

ANSWER TO A PRAYER

It was the last day of Sun Dance. The piercings were over; the dancers and supporters were happy. As I danced with the other men and women, I blew my eagle bone whistle. To tell you the truth, blowing a whistle for four days without drinking water gets really hard. Of course, we might get some gut soup one night, a traditional delicacy, but when I'd blow my whistle the next morning, my breath would go out the slot of the whistle right up my noise. It smelled awful. It took a couple of years to realize I could turn my whistle over. That was much better. But I digress. On this particular morning my thoughts drifted to what we had done and the fate of the world. So I asked whatever listens to such prayers and questions, "Will this do any good?"

At that moment I clearly heard a voice that was not mine.

It said, "Stevo."

When I hear it like that, I always pay close attention.

I said, "What?"

It replied, "It won't be as bad as it could be."

That answer has kept me going for years.

~~~~~~~~~~~~~~~~~~

Through such experiences, I realized surrender does not entail a zombie-like experience, where we are mindlessly driven by a higher hypnotic power. That was what I was afraid of. I didn't want to lose my individuality – still don't – but I confused my individuality with my ego. To surrender means to become that hollow bone, like an eagle bone whistle, a container of sacred space from which the magician's universe is employed. As Aleut elder Larry Merculieff said, "From a spiritual
~~~~~~~~~~~~~~~~~~

and physical point of view, nothing new can be created without sacred space." The more we create, the more we receive. The more we receive, the more we give back. By human standards, the universe is inexhaustible. What we gain from surrender is a greater connection with magic, not a hall pass from action. If not ready for the responsibility and greater accountability of a spiritual magician, don't surrender. Don't kick the puppy.

A "Good Hands" Story

We got out of the sweat lodge about 11 pm. A heavy, wet snow was falling. It was a usual Montana March storm, the kind that gets mooshed into slush, then compacted to ice by traffic as the temperature drops. I had about a 60 mile drive home through the blizzard and deer that roam the hills and roads between Jeffers and Bozeman. In Ennis, I slowed down for deer trotting across the street in a downtown crosswalk.

The storm worsened as I dropped over the Ennis Hill near Norris. A snowplow coming from the other direction blinded me as the slush cloud it raised plastered my windshield through the plow's dazzling headlights. Its draft almost blew my car off the road. I slowed even more, felt the tires grip and maintained control.

About fifteen miles from home with snow still falling, I suddenly saw deer on both sides of the road and in the road. I did what I often did because it keeps deer away; even insurance companies recommend it. I blew a long blast with the horn. Well, with deer on both sides of the road they didn't move in one direction when I blew the horn, as I expected. Instead, they criss-crossed all over the road. Deer ran from right to left and left to right. They ran up and down the highway. Had the car not fishtailed uncontrollably through the herd, I would have hit at least a few. And then the last doe, a big one, jumped from the right side of the road and ran in front of me. I had her. I ran over her hind left heel and spun her chest around into the driver's door.

But no! I missed her. I don't know how. It literally had to be by less than a hair.

Then I truly lost control of the car. I slid past a roadside fatality cross. The car was heading off the road and over an embankment. I remember looking at my hands thinking, 'Crap! After all that I'm going off the road now?' There was nothing I could do. I actually took my hands off the wheel.

Then something took over. Something reached around from behind me and took the wheel. I could feel "arms" around my shoulders. The car found traction and stayed on the road. I re-took the wheel and made the turn, too mystified to be in shock. That came later. I made it home, truly grateful to be in my bed and not upside down hanging by my seatbelt in a blizzard.

The words of a friend echoed in my ears as I walked in the door. "Angels surround you," she said as I left Bozeman that afternoon for the lodge. They had.

~~~~~~~~~~~~~~~~~~

I get chills whenever I think about this story. Had I not let go, I would have crashed. Had I not retaken control, I would have burned. I didn't offer bales of sage the next day in appreciation, but I had to do something. I said a lot of thank yous.

In the magical world, cause and effect are very precise. They are just not logical. To become a hollow bone we become the container of energy. Yet, that hollow bone really isn't hollow. It is the manifestation of the idea to become a clear and high-powered channel of Source energy in order to express the highest intent of our authentic self so that what is within can radiate out into the sacred space of the world. We give that energy form and direction and it does the same to us. What I surrender to is an evolving presence and a dynamic state. Sometimes I drive the car; sometimes the car drives me.

Letting Go Practice

We've all had experiences we never want to have again. Some have left us physically scarred; others mentally or emotionally battered, or spiritually stunted. When I look at why I had those experiences, especially as an adult, I have to admit I did something to bring them on. I was also incredibly lucky quite a few times, likely because of divine intervention or something similar. There's a Lakota belief that says the better you walk the Red Road, the closer the spirits stay to you to help you when you need. I'm sure they've had to sprint hard to get to me in time.

In any case, I have attitudes and behaviors I know I'd be better off without, ones that cause me to do certain things in this lifetime that can
~~~~~~~~~~~~~~~~~~

bring me repeat experiences I say I don't want to again. Or I have attitudes I know that stop me from moving from fear to love on my comfort zone spectrum. I use the following practice to help me let go of things I want to release before I die, so I don't bring them with me to wherever I may go next. Honest self-reflection sets the stage. Imagination drives the release. Whatever it is I say I don't want, I imagine myself without it. It's that simple. Then I imagine my life and me free of that and the new impacts I will have without it. The imagined life is what really anchors the release. Normally I experience a greater sense of freedom after this practice. Bit by bit, the imagined behaviors and life come into being. I feel when we talk about higher thought and higher vibration, this is a method by which to experience those, as well.

Before we start, I have a confession to make. I have a lot of self-importance, a totally illogical self-concept. I've cut it back, but it can take little to incite the return of one or more of its heads. A recent spurt of self-importance came from a personalized license plate I saw on a shiny black BMW convertible. It read UNVME. My immediate reaction to the driver was, 'What a dick.'

Rather than appreciate the creative boldness of this man's personal expression with the reactions those five letters likely cause as he drives around, including my own, I immediately felt I was better than he by assuring myself not only did I not envy him, but I would never do anything so callous. But then I reconsidered his plate and asked myself, 'Is this a command? A statement? A wish? A prediction? Maybe even a question?' His intent for his license plate doesn't matter. What matters is that it immediately reflected me to myself and created part of my reality. Not only did he apparently have more than me, he flaunted it. Yes, I did envy him. And what good could that possibly do? If a rising tide raises all boats, why did I want to be a submarine and torpedo him? Maybe because Ted Turner grants me access through his land to the wilderness and I had no idea what this guy had done for me.

However, I don't want to carry the pettiness of envy with me when I die, nor do I want to be responsible for adding it to the morphic field. As I looked into this license plate, I began to see many other people I envy. I'm not happy about it, but it's there and something I want to release. Plus, when I looked up the definition of envy and its synonyms, there was not one flattering word in the bunch. The kindest include: prejudice, malice, backbiting, resentment. Envy has a lot of heads, too.

So here we go. The suggested intent of this practice is to authentically bring a feeling into your awareness and space you want to release and release it. Begin with your preferred way of preparing yourself and your sacred space. Ask for help and health. Then do a daily review or re-experience a moment when you demonstrated a character trait you want to release. Looking up the word in the dictionary and checking a thesaurus for synonyms beforehand might help you the way it did me to better understand the depth and possible consequences of this trait. While within your space, experience the impacts this characteristic brings to you and your life. Perceive it through your heart, mind, body and spirit. Sense how it affects your interactions with others. After you experience the trait in these ways, release it from your heart, mind, body and spirit to maximize the release. The release sequence you choose is up to you.

I suggest doing this practice either the night before or the morning of a day you've picked when you will not feed the feeling you intend to release with thought or behavior. If a day is too long, then try to avoid feeding the feeling just for a morning. Do something to put yourself in a position where you will have to face this feeling and behavior, but simply let it go. Through intent, awareness and right action, you will create a higher order of authenticity that elevates you and your interactions with the world and others. The more personal the experiences are that this characteristic brings out in you, especially when you feel wronged or hurt or broken hearted, the more challenging this practice may be. Stay focused on what you really want to leave behind in this life and not carry with you into the next. That may give the impetus necessary for an authentic release, which is a relief.

Now I thank the UNVME man. He gave me such a gift. If I see him again, I'll try to stop him and shake his hand for tossing this in my face and challenging me to get over it.

~~~~~~~~~~~~~~~~~~~
~~~~~~~~~~~~~~~~~~~

16

Chaos and Order

"Sometimes I believe in as many as six impossible things before breakfast."
Alice

"That is an excellent practice."
The Mad Hatter

One of my favorite tales is Sir Gawain and the Green Knight, an Arthurian legend of renown. Spoiler alert: it matters not how much of the story I share here, as it can be read many times and still savored. One of the story's prime themes is reciprocity, but there is so much more that relates to sacred relationship. Here is a brief summary.

Once upon a time, as King Arthur and the Knights of the Roundtable and their ladies feasted in the king's great hall, a huge Green Knight rode in, bellowing a challenge to every knight of the Roundtable. Carrying a large ax, he welcomed any knight to smite his neck, on condition that that knight would ride alone to the Green Chapel one year and one day hence to receive a similar blow at the hands of the Green Knight.

Everything about the Green Knight was green, his armor, his hair, his skin, even his huge horse and its tack, with only highlights of gold threaded into each of them. The Knight stood at least a head taller than any other man anywhere and at least twice the girth. In short, he was a giant.

Arthur accepted the challenge, but his young nephew, Sir Gawain, convinced the king it was the duty of one of his knights to do so, and he humbly put himself forward as the most expendable knight of all.

With the Green Knight's huge ax in Gawain's hands, the Green Knight put his forehead and chest on the dining table and exposed the back of his massive neck by moving his thick green locks of hair to the side so Gawain could get a clear shot. With a single stroke, Gawain severed the man's head and sunk the blade deep into the table. Blood spurted as the head rolled off the table and onto the floor. The Green Knight grabbed his head and, with the head doing the talking, told Gawain he expected to see him in a year and a day to honor the agreement, lest all the tales and fables and heroic deeds of the Arthurian Court were false. With head in hand, the Green Knight saddled his horse and rode out of the hall.

During the course of the next year, Gawain, who was initially deemed unworthy for a seat at the Roundtable, was awarded every courtesy. A fortnight before it was his time to leave Camelot and search for the Green Knight, all bid him farewell. Properly attired and equipped, the young knight rode alone to his quest, in search of the Green Knight.

Gawain rode through unknown parts of the Isles, searching for the Knight. He encountered hardships and challenges and, reluctantly, slew every foe who would not let him pass. On Christmas Eve, several days before his appointment, an exhausted Gawain came upon a magnificent castle in the deep forest surrounded by a moat. He was welcomed inside and dined and entertained with excellent food, a gracious host, and the men and women of the castle. Finally his host asked Gawain why he had come that way.

Gawain related his story, said he would take gracious shelter for the night, but must be on in the morning. His host was ecstatic and said the Green Knight's abode was only a short distance away, so Gawain was welcome to recover at the castle from the travails of his quest until the morning of his appointment. Then his host would have one of his men guide Gawain to the Green Knight.

"I will be up early for the hunt tomorrow," Gawain's host said. "You must rest. When I return, I will give you everything I gained during the hunt and you will give me everything you gained during the day."

Gawain conceded to stay and accepted his host's proposal. The next morning, while the hunter was out, his extraordinarily beautiful wife stole into Gawain's chambers and awoke him, inviting him to a day of extraordinary passion. Gawain, of course, resisted, although more than tempted to a tryst, as his life would soon be over. After hours of teasing and idle chat, the hunter's wife implored Gawain for a least a kiss. He courteously complied.

When the hunter returned that evening, he gave all the meat and pelts from a good day in the woods to Gawain. Gawain gave his host a kiss, in return. The host was amused and asked Gawain from whom he got such a gift. Gawain refused to say as that was not part of the deal. His host laughed and said Gawain fared much better that day than did the hunter.

The second day the hunter rose early for the chase. A still exhausted Gawain slept until awoken by the hunter's beautiful wife. She again tempted him with all her womanly wiles and more. Gawain, again, reluctantly resisted. When it was time for her to leave, she kissed Gawain twice.

Upon his return, the hunter again gave Gawain all the spoils of the hunt. Gawain gave his host two kisses in return. More feasting ensued and Gawain slept the night away, only to be awoken a third time by the woman, whose look, looks and fragrances were more glorious than ever. She lured him with love and teased him even more in his chambers all day. Gawain was beside himself, but did not give in, even though he knew he would die in the morning.

Finally, the woman conceded and gave Gawain three kisses. This time she also unwrapped a silk scarf for a boon, telling him it will keep him from all harm. He accepted that, as well, and watched her walk away for as long as he could.

The hunter returned from his third hunt with only a single fox pelt. He gave it to Gawain, as agreed. Gawain, in turn, gave his host three courteous kisses, then the household feasted.

In the morning after a restless night awaiting execution, Gawain rose early and dressed for his appointment with the Green Knight. He put on his full battle regalia and tied the silk scarf about his arm. He rode to the Green Chapel with his host's guide. The Green Knight was in the courtyard at the grinding wheel, sharpening his blade. He brusquely commanded Gawain to put his head over a stump and expose his neck. Gawain did. The knight struck straight and hard and true, yet Gawain got but a scratch as the blade came down on his neck. Gawain jumped from the stump.

"That is for keeping the scarf," the Green Knight laughed. For he and the hunter were the same, a magical shapeshifter who was put to this task by Morgaine Le Fay, King Arthur's half-sister, sometime adversary and sometime ally. "Had you not kept it, you would not have received even a mark," the knight continued.

Afterward, the two men joked and bantered, as the single strike of the ax by each man to each man had been delivered. The moral of the story? Apart from the almost impossibly high standards Gawain held himself to as both a guest and a Knight of the Roundtable, it is also one of trust and reciprocity. Gawain initially assumed the challenge from Arthur because Arthur was his elder and mentor. Assuming the task was his way of reciprocating to Arthur for the place Arthur gave him in his household. And secondly, reciprocity to his guest…for Gawain did everything that was asked of him under the most demanding of conditions of his quest, with the minor infraction of the lady's scarf. I would have lost my head somewhere along the line.

The Green Knight allowed Gawain the scarf. The knight said it was actually his and that his wife acted on his behalf. Gawain kept the scarf as a reminder of his flaw. Whenever he felt the least bit haughty, he would look at the scarf he kept on his arm and know that he had succumbed to fear and temptation at least once, and did not wish to do it again.

So, the scarf was a gift to both Gawain's human self, as Gawain, and his knightly higher self, represented as Sir Gawain. It acknowledged the ebb and flow between our dual and all too often conflicting, rather than complementary, nature. And the scarf is a bridge, capable of bringing our selves together within the bonds of sacred space, the guest chamber in which Gawain rested and was tempted. Of course, the Green Knight's wife represents many things, including the Divine Feminine, healing grace, joy, pleasure, beauty, temptation, distraction, deception and protection.

Throughout this story, we see physical beings having a spiritual experience, spiritual beings having a physical experience and spiritual beings having a spiritual experience. These represent the three worlds: the Above, the Below and the Within. Whichever self is dominant at any time, the other self is always in the wings waiting. The higher self can delude us into thinking we are doing great things through self-denial, while at the same time the human self craves every desire. Therefore, constant vigilance is required to maintain the proper dynamic, shapeshifting balance between these two aspects of self in order to be authentic. I've always wondered what Gawain would have given his host had Gawain given in to his wife.

And trust? Where does that fit in? Obviously, Arthur trusted Gawain to fulfill his commitment to the Green Knight, as the reputation of Camelot rested with Gawain. There was never any suggestion otherwise. Gawain trusted in both his own strength and a higher power that he would find the help he needed to find the Green Chapel. He trusted in The Lady when she gave him the scarf that would protect him from all harm. Paradoxically, it was his trust in her and promise to her that resulted in the slight wound he did receive. Ultimately, it was his trust in the scarf, rather than honoring his word to his hunter host, that cost him the blood he shed. His word would have protected him more than the scarf, so he had to reciprocate for the "gift" with blood.

Temptation is rampant in this story. Gawain was tempted to not fulfill his quest in the first place. There were temptations of the Green Knight's most alluring wife and even temptation from the guide who rode with Gawain the last part of his journey who tried to dissuade Gawain from going to the Green Chapel. Unwavering intent and committed action are ways to the magic of the higher self. As long as one is compelled to do something, there will be temptation.

This quest was Gawain's Dark Night to the Underworld on his way to the Green Knight, the color of life and renewal. And, in true shamanic and heroic journey fashion, his trip back to Camelot and Arthur's Court was as full of adventure as was the journey away. His treasure, his physical take-away, was the scarf, which all the other Knights of the Round Table adopted as a reminder of their duality and fallibility. Hence, Gawain's quest elevated Arthur's knights to a higher standard of humility and accountability.

Yet it was Gawain, perhaps the least of Arthur's knights, who answered the challenge. Does that mean every knight of the Roundtable had the balls to find the Green Knight and to demonstrate that they sent the least among them, or does it mean that Gawain was the most expendable and so would be missed the least after losing his head? Or that Gawain was the bravest and most loyal to Arthur? Gawain's acceptance of the quest and his successful return put the entire Roundtable in self-reflection, especially its greatest champions – Lancelot, Galahad, Kay and Perceval.

Take a quantum leap from Arthurian Legend to a Nobel Prize Winning Chemist, Ilya Prigogine. His studies also brought two opposing views together, these of classical physics: chaos and order. Prigogine's work suggests what other scientists thought impossible – that order could come out of chaos.

Ilya Prigogine won the 1977 Nobel Prize in Chemistry for his work on the thermodynamics of non-equilibrium systems. I won't get technical but the point is that his work suggests how the two great themes of classic science, order and chaos, which coexisted uneasily for centuries for scientists *because they were simultaneously observed*, are being reconciled in a new and unexpected synthesis.

This is a game changer. Basically, Prigogine mathematically showed that when systems break down, some reorganize at a higher level, which means they can sustain a higher energetic input than before the breakdown. He and colleague Isabelle Stengers wrote *Order out of Chaos*, which details their work. Some social scientists embrace their findings because of their applicability to human systems.

Order out of chaos correlates with the self-help axiom of breakdown to breakthrough. The input of energy from an outside source enables broken systems to reorganize, otherwise entropy is irreversible. When we transform and bring energy to the planet through imagination, experiences, money, talents and creations – in other words, through action – the world changes and order can come out of chaos. However, without systemic breakdown, reorganization at a higher level seems impossible because the system is able to hang on to its current form, but it might take increasingly more energy to maintain a form that's out of date. Systemic breakdown is scary, but without it a system might repair itself and continue to function, while limping its way toward total entropy. Think of political and economic systems or human relationships as examples. Should we intend to get back to normal or intend to get better? How many myths and legends and heroic quests revolve around getting back to normal? I think we know the answer and doubt the following conversation would ever be uttered in any tale of renown or with a first grader.

Q: What do you want to be when you grow up?

A: Normal.

Q: What do you want to do when you grow up?

A: Get back to normal.

What if there is a better way?

As the legendary Phoenix nears the end of its long life, it builds a funeral pyre, *ignites it with a single clap of its wings* – which emulates the hand clap of a command – descends into flames and immolates itself into ash. In time, something stirs the ashes into life, first as an egg, then as a chick, which soon soars as the colorful avatar it is meant to be. It is and is not the same as it was before. It is reborn.

It's not that what doesn't kill us makes us stronger. It's more like what doesn't make us stronger kills us. Obviously we can break down and stay that way. Or, we can re-build from new energy. Fundamentally, these rebuilds make people more resilient to what broke them in the first place, given enough time to solidify the rebuild. During the rebuild, though, susceptibility to another breakdown is high. That is when sacred space can be a crucible of healing and a cocoon of metamorphosis.

As the Gawain and the Green Knight story elucidates, the heroic journey is a journey of breakdown through the Dark Night of the Soul to breakthrough. The secret to the success of the breakthrough is to be cognizant that the breakthrough is not just more of the same at a higher level, but a totally different way of handling energy through great awareness and right action. Paradoxically, the journey breaks us down *and* gives us what we need to break through to break free. We can't get back to normal, not even in a quantum anything-goes universe. Just as well…

Someday the heroic journey will help bring more light to the order out of chaos quandary. In the scheme of conscious evolution, everyone and everything is journeying back toward the Source and everything is temporary. So breakdown is temporary, and much of how long a breakdown lasts depends on our actions and us. As hypnotherapist Patricia Hall states, "If there is something that I want that I do not have, then there is something I do not know." This applies to wanting the Dark Night to end. We have to go through it to get out of it. As we go through it, we often stop wanting what drove us there.

The correlation between Ilya Prigogine's work and the Dark Night of the Soul is that breakdown is natural. It is a requisite for our evolutionary journey. Without sacred space we may break down and stay down. Within sacred space we pull it together, recover, re-assemble, re-organize, get up, and, if we do this with the conscious intent of not just appreciation but self-reflection and evaluation, the journey will extend in multiple directions. It will take us to the below and inward to recover our soul or discover any other revelatory treasure, then bring us back to the light and beyond, dispelling victim consciousness for hero consciousness. In the end, we are able to handle a greater energetic input and capable of the greater energetic output of right action.

The Gawain Practice

This exercise intends to lead you on a journey of fulfillment, during which you will ask for and receive a gift of ayni, which you will manifest and offer in sacred reciprocity to the 3D world. In other words, you will journey to the spirit world to receive a gift you will leave as an offering to the physical world for something you have already received. For example, I saw a friend recently who was absolutely distraught over her missing dog. I told her things would work out and her dog was not swept away by the high water in the creek nearby, as she feared. I prayed for her dog's safe return. I called my friend this morning. She told me her dog had made it home, but without her collar, so she probably had been stuck somewhere. I did the following practice to learn what I could leave in appreciation for the safe return of my friend's dog.

Prepare yourself through relaxed and deep breathing and activate your sacred space with smudging and sound, either following earlier suggestions or what you have adapted that works for you. Move the heart. Still the mind. Then voice your request. Ask to be given what it is you are to give in return for something you have already received. Be clear with this intent, as you will repeat it later.

Now, with that intent clearly given, perceive yourself to be along a warm beach of a river. Not far from you is a cliff or hill with a cave. Walk to the cave, being mindful of why you are there. Carry a very strong feeling of gratitude with you as you go inside. Walk inside the cave a bit and, when you can no longer see the entrance, sit by a small, bright fire in a part of the cave with a high ceiling. Take something you have with you and leave at the fire as an offering. Again, voice your request for something you are to be given and reinforce your feeling of appreciation. Sit there quietly at the fire with your hands and heart receptive. Gaze into the fire. Notice the firelight and shadows on the walls and ceiling.

In time, a figure will come to you and leave you something. It will either be left with you or you may get an image or idea of what is appropriate ayni for what you have received. Say your thanks and walk out of the cave.

From the beach see yourself sitting at your sacred space in 3D world. Allow your journey body to fully integrate with your 3D body. When you are ready, slowly open your eyes.

Remember to give away what you receive in the cave.

Variation: Rather than going to a cave and waiting to be given something, you can open a chest and look inside for your offering, or open a door and go into a room to find or be given an offering, or dive into a shipwreck, or any other variation you want and offer whatever you find as your ayni.[15]

~~~~~~~~~~~~~~~~~~~~~

[15] A more detailed recording of this and other meditative practices are available from www.steveguettermann.com.
~~~~~~~~~~~~~~~~~~~~~

17

Self-activation

"Curiosity killed the cat, but satisfaction brought it back."
Titusville Herald Newspaper, December 23, 1912

There are two basic types of questioning. The first is what I call beta questioning, embodied in finger-nail biting anxious, indecisive, low-amplitude thought patterns of "Should I?" or "Shouldn't I?" as in "Go or get off the pot." Then there is theta questioning. This type of questioning engages when one is confronted with mystery and creation, or it is spawned via meditation and contemplation, observation and investigation. It's said there is no such thing as a stupid question, but I'm not so sure. So maybe there are three types.

Sacred reciprocity leads to theta questioning. A good question can show profound curiosity and understanding. I know. I've written it's better to get over things than to understand them, but that was a metaphor meaning don't stand under the influence of things that we are better off getting over. Reciprocity leads into mystery and creation. These encounters give fodder for meditation and contemplation and the impetus to ask "Why?" and "Why not?" and questions that seek truth and question what is held to be true. A good question opens a larger world, not a world where the decisions are about whether to go to the mall or the movies, or whether to get a hamburger or Chinese food.

When Jack Schwarz was a little Dutch boy growing up in Holland, he was told to not stomp through the water behind the dikes because his shoes and knee socks would get wet and he'd catch a cold sitting in school all day with wet clothes. He wanted to find out if that was true. So Jack stomped through scores of puddles on his way to school, then dutifully sat at his desk with wet clothes on. He did not catch a cold.

Next, he questioned that he had to eat three times a day. Jack never ate much, not even as a child. So, when forced to eat when he did not want, he'd make himself throw up when he was alone. He felt better when he did not eat three times a day. Once again, he found what he was told was not true for him.

Sleeping eight hours a day did not work for him either, no matter how well he was tucked in. He was rested with two hours or less and functioned fine. Jack's type of question and answer *experiences* developed his own authority and authenticity, and permission to pursue his personal mission. He claimed this had much to do with his abilities to perceive human energies, be an intuitive and heal himself quickly from physical injury. "God does not love me more than he loves you," he used to joke when people said he was lucky because of these abilities.

We should be encouraged to question what we are told. If we are not, then it could be a sign that what we are told is not true or whoever is telling us something really doesn't know why they are saying it. If what we are told is true, there is no harm in questioning. There is much greater harm not questioning, especially when what is demanded of us has no basis, but we do it anyway. We harm each other and ourselves with that kind of doing.

"Good question!" is a great compliment. A good question stimulates intuition, invites investigation and rewards curiosity without killing the cat or kicking the puppy. A good question keeps us open to change and makes new connections into realms of possibility. A good question excites sacred space, the vibrational response to an endorphin rush. A good question attracts a good answer. A good answer strengthens relationship and sanctifies the space in which it is received.

A person can be quite satisfied being in the flow – which paradoxically is not the path of least resistance in the actual sense. Being in the flow and authentic and true to oneself makes life more interesting, not easier. Sure, things might get a little rough for awhile if we really say or do what we feel, but once it's out in the open, we'll feel better. That means we live better.

Or does it? Being in the flow means we are in sacred relationship with the moment. It does not mean we are immune from getting bumped, bruised, buffeted, badgered, bewildered, beleaguered, beat up and befuddled. Being in the flow usually means we are doing more. When we do more, more happens. When more happens, more can go wrong. When it does, we tend to attract more attention from whom and what is around us. As Jim Miller said, "If you ain't breaking anything, you ain't doing anything."

So does being authentic and in the flow demand more than they give? Life didn't seem to work out too well for Socrates, Martin Luther King, Joan of Arc or Crazy Horse. Nazis tortured Jack Schwarz. Gawain came back with his head, six kisses – which he gave away – and a scarf. Was that enough for what he went through? Good question. But we have to do something. So we should intend that whatever we do and whatever it gives us in return – because it will give us a return – should be worth all the hell it takes to get it. So, let's go together on a little allegorical canoe trip to get a close-up of what this thing called flow is.

Imagine paddling along when a sudden situation around a river bend grabs your attention. The canoe lunges forward into the current. We are in the flow, gaining speed into the unknown. We decide to take:

Option #1 – Paddle

Things move more quickly down the path of least resistance. If anything, even more is demanded because of how fast we move in the line of the flow. It can take us over the falls, under a deadfall, or into the rocks. Natural barriers are some of the most confusing things in life. We think we're in the flow, but things are not going well. Why is it so hard? The stream is braided. Maybe we're in the wrong channel. We have to take action. We paddle.

A fast current we seem unable to escape could represent a learning experience we should recognize, but do not, or do recognize, but do not respond soon enough. Maybe we ignored or missed something subtle, such as an intuitive impulse, and are driven into a repeated experience, like that second marriage, new job or promising employee that won't work out. Obstacles may be a test or a result of not paying close enough attention to cues as to how the stream really flows. We'd give anything to know where we are going or change course, but either seems nearly impossible.

What to do? Maybe back paddle? We can go against the current at any angle we are strong enough to counter. That might be good for a while. However, short of re-enacting the Lewis & Clark Expedition, don't spend a lot of time and energy going against the current. Pull in. Survey the stream from the bank. If necessary, portage around the obstacle or to another channel, then get back in the river. A new perspective may help us realize being in the flow is not a free and easy ride to our destination. And it may help us get over things, such as a snag, rather than pinned under them. Be like the river: playful, but play for keeps.

If the speed and direction of the current are more than you can handle and leave you pummeled and stranded, chances are you need a teacher, guide or partner to help you. You may find a teacher who has been through it and willing to help you without taking over, who challenges you without abandoning or abusing you. Prepping yourself through sacred reciprocity within sacred space may sensitize you to your sensei. Good teachers will benefit from a relationship with you, as you will with a good teacher, and that is a teacher who is not in it solely for personal gain at the expense of another. Paradox is one thing; half-truths and double standards are something else.

Some people have questionable experiences with "teachers." Notorious examples abound. I have a healthy distrust of people who claim to be teachers, especially manipulative teachers of consciousness. There are also many good teachers. With that said, I offer these humble guidelines to anyone looking for a teacher.

Sense for someone authentic, present and with presence, commitment, compassion, respect, a palpable, loving reciprocal relationship to you, the planet and the stars, and an astute repertoire of practical knowledge and wisdom – all in a humorous, fun loving, insightful and adventurous package. By being present, I mean that when s/he talks with you, s/he really talks with you and listens. There is no distraction. When s/he works with you, s/he works with you. Again, there is no distraction, no sense s/he would rather be somewhere else doing something else. Also, if this person has students or helpers around, observe how everyone interacts with one another. You should feel good in their presence and resonate with the message and the method.

These suggestions may help you find an authentic teacher for yourself. That is a person who has no motive for teaching you other than a passionate commitment to you learning for your conscious evolution. This is why students are so grateful to their teachers and why the bond between student and teacher grows over time. Through a passionate commitment to you, the teacher also serves him/herself. I think that's as it should be.

So, will the teacher show up when the student is ready? I don't know. I do know the student will show up when the teacher is ready.

Let's get back to the water with…

Option #2 – Rechannel

If being in the flow seems to ask too much of us, we can rechannel the stream and try to make it flow where and how we want. The Universal Environmental Protection Agency might question our intentions. The Cosmic Corps of Engineers won't help either. If anything they might work like mad to stop us. Nevertheless, stream channelization is a high energy endeavor and takes a lot of work. It is not the path of least resistance as the existing stream is already in the path of least resistance. That is the nature of the flow. In other words, if we try to mold reality to our will rather than trusting what is and using what we are to get where we need to go, we will likely get worn out, beaten up, tossed on the rocks, impoverished, immobilized and be more unsuccessful and unhappy in more ways than going with the flow could ever do.

In other words, it's too much work with nothing to gain. Look at it this way. We co-create reality, but we really are too small to alter the universal flow. What chance do we have? None. What other choices do we have? Several, but none are very good. Our greatest gains come from giving ourselves permission to pursue and express our potentials…in accordance with the flow. It's really that simple. Finding our purpose is key. Although being in the flow is no panacea, being out of the flow is no picnic. Here's a hint on how to tell the difference between the two. When we are in the flow, our path hits us where we need to be hit, then gives us what we need to get over it. When we are out of the flow, we just keep getting hit.[16]

Ayni is in the flow. Ayni builds intuitive sensitivity in body, heart, spirit, mind and soul to help guide us, if by no other way than by mak-

---

[16] How do we know our heart's purpose? It partly comes from asking, "Am I willing to do this for ten, fifteen or twenty difficult years with little or no reward, yet do whatever it takes to be successful, including foregoing distraction and social pressure?" If the answer is yes, we might be on to something.

ing us more astute observers of nature and enjoying the moment, being cognizant of what that expression feels like. Can you be in the flow and an obstacle to the expression of others if that is your purpose? That's possible. You can also be an obstacle *and* the answer to someone's prayers. It's all part of the process. Sooner or later, the natural flow overcomes all obstacles...rebuilding the channel here, dismantling it there...washing away barriers over there. Life's creative cycles trump repetition. The repeat of seasons bring familiarity as well as newness, another reason why no man can step into the same river twice. Let it go. Let it flow. Appreciate the obstacles. Experienced paddlers don't take obstacles personally. They simply are. Obstacles are often there for reasons we neither see nor understand, nor may it be our purpose to do so. (I no longer recommend asking the Great Mysterious to show itself, for instance.) But they do serve a purpose and are a pervasive and necessary part of returning to Source. Overcoming them is the essence of physical life. The ocean refuses no river. The flow refuses no explorer.

But all these obstacles can make us long for...

Option #3 – Quit

We can get out of the river and hitch a ride back to the car. That is safe...and boring. Sometimes we need a reprieve, but as a way of life, it isn't much of one. Nothing fear-based is. Paddlers also know eddies and pockets of dead water can be great places to rest, but not in which to subsist. And it can take a lot of effort to get out of one. Choose your eddies carefully.

It is scary to go with the flow when one has a family and obligations. Yet if we live true to ourselves first, and then demonstrate this to our children, and study and learn from role models who resonate with our heart and purpose, what presents itself to us is infinitely more exciting and sustaining. Verve will serve us infinitely more abundantly than anything less because what appears to be safe, if it is outside the flow, never is. Compromise after you've found your purpose, not before. A planet of purposeful purpose-pursuing people is a planet whose time has come. But don't trust me on this. Trust yourself.

Still, there is always the temptation to take...

Option #4 – Build a bridge

Some people who sit outside of the flow may think things look better on the other side of the stream and want to build a bridge. It might be a toll bridge; it might be a troll bridge. Think of bridge building as a way of letting materialism keep us from our purpose. We build a bridge to get to the other side of the stream, only to find that things are much the same over there. The grass was greener, until the bridge. The bridge building continues as does the stream, but the two never, ever meet. We look down to the stream as we cross the bridge, wondering what it would be like to be on the water. The water calls to us much louder than the bridge does. What do we do? At the very least, we need to know how to swim because that bridge won't last forever. The best reason for a bridge is to get us to a place where we can get down to the water and into the flow. So, is building the bridge enabling or disabling? We should answer that before doing anything. A bridge takes us to a destination. A river takes us on a journey.

If a bridge seems too benign, we may choose...

Option #5 – Build a dam

What's a river without a dam? Free. Once there's a dam a river is no longer a river. Fascinating that our arteries became more blocked as more dams were built and now as dams are slowly being dismantled in some parts of the world, some people's arteries are clearing. Coincidence? I don't think so. And remember the mention of sand wars in Chapter 7? One reason the world is fighting over sand is because dams are holding it back so ocean beaches are not being replenished by sand from free flowing rivers.

What do dams do literally? One biggie is flood control. What do dams do metaphorically? Flow control. Flood control is flow control. Flood control sounds good until we realize the vital importance floods play in ecosystem balance. Flooding is the river equivalent to a forest fire. It's cleansing, necessary for health and for regeneration. Civilizations were built upon acknowledging, using and thanking rivers for flooding. Floods also restore ground water, which can be thought of as our subconscious resources. While it is true that in some years floods reach higher and take more than others, losses can be mitigated by not building too low in the floodplain. Letting a river flow free means it will run wild from time to time. That's a benefit, not a crime. When there are losses, communities can do what we do now...help each other. On the other hand, building right on a riverbank and expecting the house to be safe because there's a dam upstream is not for the greatest good.

Metaphorically, it is impossible to be in the flow when paddling behind a dam. There is little benefit to controlling a journey by stopping its flow. Who would ever go to a movie titled: *A River Doesn't Run Through It?* The Cosmic Corps of Engineers won't like this either and will work hard to stop us from stopping it. Even Helen Keller saw it and said, "Security is mostly a superstition. It does not exist in nature, nor do the children of men as a whole experience it. Avoiding danger is no safer in the long run than outright exposure. Life is either a daring adventure, or nothing."

So yep, make changes. Do something. But if that something changes the flow of what is meant to be, question it. When we dam a river we damn ourselves. Sooner or later that dam is going to go and come hell or high water, we'll have to ride it out then.

This brings us to…

Option #6 – Take a ferry

I love old time ferries where I get pulled across the river on a barge attached to a riverbank cable. They are getting harder to find, though. Metaphorically, ferry crossings are little different than crossing a stream on a bridge, although they get us closer to the water.

Operating a river ferry can be transcendental. One of my favorite parts in Herman Hesse's classic book, *Siddhartha,* is when Siddhartha becomes a ferryman with Vasudeva. Hesse writes that one day Siddhartha realizes the river exists only in the now and everywhere at once: upstream, downstream, at the sea and at the source. He realizes that his existence as a boy, an old man and everything in between are not separate. He, the river and everything in life exist only in the omnipresent. Why does the ferryman never get bored doing what seems to be the same thing everyday? Because the river is never the same and it's always present. The ferryman is attuned to this and to the comparable evolution of himself with all that is. But one does not need to be a ferryman or any specific thing to have this connection. Nonattachment to what we do and are is a true gift from the connected universe.

"So," a person may ask, "if everything is connected and perfect, what is wrong if I sit on the bank, cross a stream via a bridge, or any number of other things I can do in and with life in or out of the water?"

Nothing. I merely suggest we give back to everything that allows us to be and to do and exercise our free will in ways that do not impose our will upon the river's, but rather in ways that compose our will. Then we experience greater magic because that is how life thanks us for our thanks. It's more fun that way. Desperate times do not call for desperate measures. They call for magical ones.

Sacred reciprocity is with the flow. When we are in there and living right, the planet does not have to use as much energy to sustain us. That is a wonderful way to reciprocate. In this way, ayni adds to natural capital. Ayni also helps us avoid placing recurring emotional burdens on the planet by allowing for their release and transformation…when done consciously. The good that does extends deeply into us, into sacred space and the energy of the planet, as well. We give more so need less, and so we have more.

It's hard to understand when cultures and ways of life that understand the balance of giving and receiving are crushed by cultures that don't. People of the dominant cultures seldom experience, yet alone understand, the truths and losses of indigenous people. However, we are all indigenous. And as we are all indigenous, without that balance we not only crush the dreams of life, we crush our dreams of dreams. But through dreaming, our dreams can be restored.

The universe is not a sporadic, fickle and conditional provider, unless that's what we make it. To try to fetter the universe with conditions of how desires will be satisfied, or how goals will be attained is as mindless as trying to push or dam(n) the river. Mindfulness helps us know what to ask for, how to ask for it, and how to use the creative flow for our fulfillment to allow right thought, word and action for intended manifestation. The less ego and the more heart in ayni, the more magical the result.

Although we may behave as if we can operate outside of the principles of the universe, we really can't, at least not in the long term. Universal oneness will inevitably include us. We have a choice: flow now or flow later. We can resist kicking and screaming, and grab on to any distraction we create or are not strong enough to resist, or we can flow with the intent to become ever more mindful of the mysterious and creative forces of an ever-increasing expansive universe, and use them for the highest and greatest good. Paradoxically, these collective forces become a synergistic force that does not force. It enables and allows. I call this the Paradox of Power. It has to do what we want; we have to do what it wants. Our sacred space behaves the same way, incorporating more creative, volitional and non-volitional energies as it expands.

Omnipresent and omnipatient, this force is also a creative potential that enables expansion through thought, word and form. The paradox of potential is that we can never reach it. As we pursue potential, it expands and so do we. The universe seems to become more full of potential as it expands, too, filling with more dark matter and dark energy. Dark energy may be consciousness itself, becoming ever more conscious of itself, intending to create more of itself. So, why is the universe expanding? It chooses to. We can do the same with sacred space, filling it with the high amplitude energies of love, life, consciousness, imagination, intent, appreciation and whatever else we choose.

18

Meeting Quetzalcoatl

"Late in the night, I seemed to commune with entities of pure thought, beaming a message at me. Their words hovered in my mind, then scattered away. I retrieved my notebook and scrawled them down before they vanished from my memory. 'You go deeper into the Physical to get to the Infinite.'"
Daniel Pinchbeck – 2012: The Return of Quetzalcoatl

Our time has many names, including New Age, Aquarian Age, Information Age and Computer Age. Whatever we call it, it seems to be a Coming of Age age. Change comes fast. We seem to be moving toward something positive, but that is precariously balanced with the Holocene Age of Extinction, which is the sixth great extinction many anthropologists and other scientists say is the current age. The Holocene is also known as the Age of Man. So to tip the scales in our favor, we need to move toward the Age of Universal Man, *Homo universalis*, as Barbara Marx Hubbard says, which is an age of conscious evolution rather than conscious extinction. We can start this move by realizing that not only do we lose a species in extinction, we lose its voice, its language, its way to communicate and its connection with the universe. That language is not only a gift from the Imaginator/Imaginatrix to that species, it is also a gift to us as we learn how each species perceives and interacts with the world.

Some human language originated from sounds heard in nature, onomatopoeic sources, an ongoing orchestration of natural sound and vibration, especially from animals. Language will not evolve in the way it can when we no longer hear such sounds. I heard this in a catbird's song one morning as I walked along Winter Ouzel Creek near my home. When birds and whales and frogs and crickets sing with all they've got, despite all that goes on around them, I sense how much they are doing to maintain the purity and evolution of the planet simply with their song. As biologist E.O. Wilson asks, "Do we really want to live on a planet where one species cannot leave half of it for the other 8.9 million species?" If we can leave half the planet in tact, we may shapeshift into what don Oscar recommends: "...rather than being a dominating species we become an altruistic, interdependent presence within the great web of life." This can reverse the Holocene Age of Extinction and enhance the Age of Man.

Animal sounds became shamanic songs to call in animal allies – from this world and beyond. Now languages are lost through extinction. It is not just plants, animals, fungi and human cultures that are leaving. It is their language, gifts, perceptions and wisdom. So we are left with less understanding of the natural world and a lessened opportunity to understand it because the orchestra is not complete. We originated within a symphony, but are forced to live in a cacophony. As the natural world becomes less diverse, it is less communicative, knowledgeable, wise and beautiful as strands of the web of life are cut and lost. We are engaged in a biological book burning and censorship, not just heralding a Silent Spring, but a Silent Millennium. Is this really the legacy of the Age of Man? Much of the natural world hides from us, fearing we will find it. The planet still loves us as one of her own, but the reciprocity and decisions of the natural world are becoming like ours, based on fear rather than love. There is a difference between Pachamama and the natural world – Pachamama contains the natural world, but there is more to her than that. Her consciousness is distinct from, but connected to, everything that lives here.

Beauty. Species. Sound. All being lost. Going...going...almost gone. Sacred space can help create a refuge for these diminishing connections to the higher realms. I know these magnificent creatures do not want to leave us or the planet. They don't want to exist just in the ethers. They want to live here.

Some human behaviorists suggest we are attracted to beauty because we equate beauty with health. Beauty is a transformational and inspirational vibration. As the beauty and the diversity of life on our planet diminish, we don't have beauty available to us to transcend and transform our consciousness. Without a foundation of natural beauty, it's harder for us to recover once we get knocked down, so we stay stuck and we stay down. For sustenance, we prey on each other instead of praying with each other. Relatively speaking, things not in balance require more to subsist than those in balance.

The natural world of creative growth and evolution is orchestrated through the mantras of our animal allies and compadres. That is what a consistent nature song is, a mantra. They are beautiful and sacred sounds used as an object of concentration and embodying some aspect of spiritual power. There is not just a predator-prey relationship...we seem to have reduced the natural world to that, being the reductionists we are. The natural world is a shapeshifting cosmology of energy and consciousness through an evolutionary flow through consciousness. To experience this may be why we're here. I like to think we are walking into the unknown every step of the way. If so, the unknown is something with which we should be intimately familiar. The purpose of ayni is to enter into sacred and appreciative relationship with the seen and unseen worlds that maintain life. From relationship to connection, from connection to expansion and from expansion to a higher vibration – which happens every step of the way – ayni may lead to a quantum jump to greater and clearer manifestation from the love and joy of being and becoming. I suspect that ayni will be appreciated and reciprocated in higher vibrational experiences, so it makes sense to learn it and practice it here.

3D reality is a difficult and beautiful place. Earth is our mystery school in which we experience cause and effect, and learn how to manifest desire in sacred relationship within sacred space. Were we to be placed in a place where manifestation of desire happens effortlessly without first learning to be responsible with this power, god only knows what we would do. So maybe the Imaginator/Imaginatrix knows what s/he is doing after all. An Age of Universal Man can be the time to remember our source, history and creative and loving power and how to use it. If we can effectively and compassionately manifest on the earth plane – by all accounts the most difficult plane of all – the joy and freedom awaiting us in more etheric realms must truly be remarkable. But first we have to know the joy and freedom that wait for us here. A Holocene Age won't help.

According to Mayan elder Hunbatz Men, going deeply into Mayan culture and ceremony activates memory, which is why learning foundational ceremony can be helpful to us all. He also said the sun activates memory. The question is, "Is this memory in everyone's DNA or the DNA of just some of us?" Well, as we are all indigenous, we all have a cultural memory of rituals, even if we have not been taught it. It is waiting to be activated through the right teacher, right action and the right states of mind and heart. According to Men that cultural memory, "does not have pollution." So, it can be Mayan memory, Druid Memory, Egyptian memory, Zulu memory. You get the idea. It is still in there. I think even languages can be resurrected from memory and dream. That would take a lot of work, but there is no reason why not. Still, if the natural world is disemboweled, it is much more difficult to activate these things. We simply have no idea what is being forgotten...or at least very deeply hidden.

DNA is our genetic code of development and behavior. As is everything, it's energy. As a conscious and physical being, Pachamama has a genetic code, which is her originating potential. What may be happening as we tap into the energy of Pachamama during this transformational time is this: for Pachamama to make her transformation to the next dimensions, she is activating new and unused energetic potential. As she brings the activation of these new codes to us from deep within herself, we share in this transformation. This is may be beyond uniting the Sacred Masculine and the Sacred Feminine. Or, it may be how it is done. I don't know. The activation of these codes for Pachamama will result in such things as her being able to overcome the effects of nuclear radiation and other toxins. The planetary upheavals we see and experience are not just her response to manmade and natural pressures and not just a detox. It is part of her activation of new codes. As we embody and assimilate her wisdom and activation by resonating with her higher vibrations we can consciously enable the activation of our own DNA, aiding planetary healing through our own. Some of this human potential is known as kundalini energy, symbolized as a coiled serpent said to reside at the base of the spine. Volumes are written and intense practices developed about this energy, so the reader is encouraged to follow up, if interested.

But there is even more. New energies are also coming to our planet from without, most notably from what astronomers call the Milky

Way's galactic sun and what the Maya call the Galactic Butterfly. This is a black hole in the center of our galaxy about 26,000 light years away, through what we know as the constellation Sagittarius. It is interesting that although a black hole purportedly allows no light to escape, although Stephen Hawking theorizes that is not true, there is energy coming to the earth from this one. This is a rare galactic phenomenon. In other words, it's uncommon for a galaxy to have a black hole in its center. And yes, although 26,000 light years away, the Maya did and do know of its existence, something our astronomers did not discover until the 1930s. The "discovery" was a result of laying transatlantic communication cable, which began to act as an antenna. The cable began to pick up signals from the cosmos. This led to research that verified the existence of the Galactic Butterfly.

In essence, at this cusp of human evolution, we have three "new" energy sources on which to draw: the higher vibration of the Earth; the energy of the galactic sun and through these and our own developing state of consciousness, the activation of more of our DNA. We also have our planetary sun. The human genome project shows there is a lot of unused DNA in our genetic makeup. It is currently called junk DNA, but the use of that term is fading, as new research provides more insight into more of what our DNA does and its potential. For those who choose, the Age of Universal Man can be the assimilation of new energies that activate new potentials that yield new expressions, which is conscious human evolution. I like to think of this as growing a new branch on the evolutionary Tree of Life. It's all energy and it's our choice as to whether or not we partake of its fruit, as well as become that fruit. Sacred reciprocity within the crucible of sacred space makes resonance with higher realms and assimilation of higher energies possible. What are these higher energies? Love, peace, compassion, kindness and how we put them into action. Ayni is a cause and an effect of human evolution. The choice is clear: we can grow new Hydra heads, spawned out of fear, or new fruitful branches on the Tree of Life, which come from our higher emotions and interactions. The latter choice awakens us to greater potential and awareness through existing, but dormant, genetic codes or through mutations, some of which are brought about by the higher vibrations of consciousness. So which came first, activating dormant DNA or higher vibrations of consciousness? I don't know. They could be the same thing. What we understand and perceive is always impacted by our state of consciousness.

The science of epigenetics, which literally means "above the gene," proposes that we pass along more than DNA in our genes; it suggests that our genes can carry memories. The Academy of Pediatrics reports that the way genes work in our bodies determines neuroendocrine structure and is strongly influenced by experience. Neuroendocrine cells help the nervous and endocrine systems work together to produce a response. Trauma experienced by earlier generations can influence the structure of our genes, making them more likely to switch on negative responses to stress and trauma. If that's true, genes must carry good memories, too, and are more likely to switch on positive responses to positive experiences.

Our DNA code may be fixed for life, but the epigenome is flexible. Epigenomes react to signals, such as diet, stress, words and others. A flexible epigenome allows us to adapt to changes and to learn from our experiences. This happens both singularly and collectively. Russian researchers apparently have discovered that DNA can even create magnetized wormholes, under the right conditions[17].

So, when we talk about conscious evolution, it is not just a state of mind. It actually can have physiological ramifications based on our experiences, as suggested in the Academy of Pediatrics report mentioned earlier. As we choose certain behaviors, let's say ceremonial experiences, these outside influences impact the structure of our genes, activating new potentials and responses. Conscious evolution happens by choice. When we make decisions and take actions from love rather than fear, those decisions impact our evolutionary, revolutionary and reactionary behavior in ways that keep us in a higher vibration, activating even more of our new potentials and resonating with new potentials of the planet. We co-create and co-evolve within an expanding sacred space that resonates with a consciously evolving planet, if I may be so bold as to suggest that. That sacred space and frame of mind are like Gawain's scarf. We can take it with us wherever we go, and maybe others will adopt it for and adapt it to themselves.

---

[17] *Vernetzte Intelligenz* (Networked Intelligence), by Grazyna Gosar and Franz Bludorf explain these connections.

Physical reality is not an illusion. It is a 3D description of processes we perceive. Quantum physics suggests reality is a cluster of possibilities, happening according to what is observed moment-by-moment. Even objects are energetic events in progress. So we have imagination and a reality – comprised of energy – manifested as a physical description of emotion-based experiences and interpretations, interdependent and acting upon one another moment-by-moment with every possibility there for the making and taking and every past, present and future moment eternally held within the energy field of the cosmos. Most of us are governed by the quirks of our physical dimension, which we call reality. For example, we get hungry and thirsty, so we eat and drink. Imagining we aren't hungry or thirsty only lasts so long…for most of us. We have to do something. Sensation stimulates action, and may be why we tend to move away from pain rather than toward pleasure.

This is the playground of sacred space. We may think we all live in the same world, but the world is not the same for any of us. It may be that there is little difference – as well as powerful connections - among what is real, what is perceived, what is imagined and what is experienced. It doesn't take much insight to realize these ingredients possess infinite possibilities of expression when mixed within the matrix of our individual consciousnesses and position in time, space and culture. Maybe there is no such thing as ordinary reality, as reality is different for each of us. Maybe there's only non-ordinary reality. Considering how things can be on Earth, that is a possibility. Our realities connect, so we share a modicum of agreement about what is, but they never completely overlap. To truly understand someone, I have to understand his or her imagination.

Both sacred space and reality are crucibles of awareness. Everything may have awareness, but not everything has volition. Actions and intent can put non-volitional energy into a creative synergy, but first we have to activate its potential. I sense that within each crucible there are both volitional and non-volitional energies. In other words, there is non-volitional energy awaiting something to put it into motion, like a rock on a hill waiting to be pushed, and volitional energy. Volitional energy represents the flow and can be thought of as the self-serving and self-initiated creative, dice-throwing movements of the universe, which, paradoxically, respond to how we throw the dice. Each throw of the dice can be a win-win, if that's what we choose to make it through non-attachment. However, seen and unseen conscious entities also have volition. Their actions impact us whether we know it or not and whether they intend it or not. We are interdependent and connected co-creators, after all. We throw and we flow. I still don't know if it's complex beyond measure or so simple it needs no measure. The following "equation" is how I explain it to myself.

Sacred space + sacred reciprocity + authenticity = Magic.

Volitional energy creates on its own and impacts our experiences. Creating sacred space for sacred reciprocity is a way for us to get to know volitional energy, befriend it and co-create. We change each other. Despite traditional science believing the energetic field around us is too weak to impact anything, quantum physics experiments *prove* we are in a participatory universe and so "good science" requires double and triple blinds to stop researcher and subject influence. So I ask again: why does science defend its own recalcitrance when faced with experimental evidence that contradicts its beliefs? Why do any of us do that?

How our combined energies show up and shapeshift may vary considerably from our imagination. Volitional energies connected with us may have imagination, too. Consequently, our volitional energy requires us to have a certain mindset, focus and behavior, which is rooted in our feeling and amplitude. That's why trust, awareness, clarity and focus are required when Pachamama and the world reciprocate to us for our ayni with their magic. So, if science acknowledges that a researcher's ideology can influence experimental results, why can't a morphic field influence our genetic code? These two things seem very similar, as science does not say exactly when a researcher's ideology influences results. Is it before, during or after the researcher is thinking about what he thinks?

We can be overcome by either inertia or flow, meaning nonvolitional or volitional energy. Or we can incite one or both to support our actions through our will. On the other hand, I suppose they can involve each other and leave us out. But these three energy types – volitional, nonvolitional and human - come together within the foundation of sacred space. Be ready. There is cause and effect; it just may not be logical. Sacred space helps us be sensitive to appropriately using the magic given us in return for ayni. Sacred space. Won't hurt anything.

The Oxford Dictionary defines archetype as "a recurrent symbol or motif in literature, art or mythology." It is considered to be a first form, a 'primal message carried in the collective unconscious. In Jungian psychology, it is a collectively inherited unconscious idea, pattern of thought, image, or concept that is universally present in individual psyches. This definition seems to support the concept of a morphic field, the Akashic Records, Teilhard de Chardin's Noosphere or any other theorized field in which thought, experience and possibility are contained.

The Hero's Journey, which I also call the heroic journey, is one of these archetypes. Archetypes embodied within it include: the hero/heroine, mentor, villain, temptation, the underworld and more. As consciousness evolves, the heroic journey steps out of myth onto life's center stage for all of us. The sacred reciprocity required from the hero or heroine for what is received is the catapult to a new stage and age of growth and action. There will always be challenges and obstacles to the gifts of knowledge, which we may not appreciate until we get over them and come out the other side. But as the nature of the gifts and our purpose for pursuing them changes, so does the nature of the obstacles. Activating these gifts activates The Self, which is achieved through purposeful and intentional reciprocity, and can transform redundant cycles of life and karma into spirals of kaleidoscopic protean expression and understanding. We stand on the threshold of newness and uniqueness. Each aspect of shapeshifted awareness is used to feel and be present as the underlying foundation of creation is experienced at the same time. It is simply a matter of consciously applying attention and intention to ayni as we move along our unique and heroic journey.

Certain archetypes are quite prevalent in the myths we weave into life. Among the most common is the death and rebirth of the hero, including Osiris, (Egyptian) Christ (European), the Phoenix (Greek, Chinese, many others) and Quetzalcoatl (Mesoamerican). There are others in almost every culture. Joseph Campbell's seminal book, *The Hero with a Thousand Faces,* highlights many of them, elucidating the hero's journey and the reborn hero as archetypes. The hero is typically reborn at what can be referred to as a higher consciousness or higher level of energy. And the hero is a male, which Campbell claims was because in earlier times it was felt females did not need to go through the trials. That concept is changing, too.

Because of its symbolism, let's briefly look at the story of Quetzalcoatl. Quetzalcoatl and his twin brother, Xoloti, came into being through virgin birth to the goddess, Coatlicue. Quetzalcoatl is Aztec for feathered serpent. He is known by other names throughout Mesoamerica, most notably Kukulkan by the Maya.

The earliest known recording of the deific feathered serpent is at the Olmec site of La Venta built in 900 B.C. At this time the feathered serpent was just that, a feathered serpent. Trade spread the acceptance of this deity across Mesoamerica and beyond. Each culture took the original myth and transformed it to suit their milieu. Quetzalcoatl's earliest astronomical association is with the Pleiades. The Pleiades were known as the serpent's rattle, and the astronomical movement of the Pleiades into alignment with the zenith sun evoked the image of a flying serpent. The Maya were first to make Quetzalcoatl/Kukulkan human. Hence, Quetzalcoatl was not just a creation god; he is also an evolutionary, shapeshifting god.

Although the story varies a bit among Mesoamerican cultures, Quetzalcoatl was considered the god of the morning star. His brother Xoloti was the evening star. Part of Quetzalcoatl's heroic journey included going to the underworld and creating the people of this age. Quetzalcoatl gave the people maize (corn), and he was sometimes a symbol of death and resurrection. He was connected to the wind, merchants, and arts and crafts, and the patron god of the priesthood and sacred knowledge, which he disseminated through books and calendars.

As Feathered Serpent, Quetzalcoatl symbolizes our god within. Feathers represent the transcendence of physical limits. Birds move between the worlds of air, earth, and for some, water. To many cultures, the serpent represents the kundalini energy coiled at the base of our spine. A feathered serpent represents the realized being, one who has appropriately activated and elevated the vital energy within as an expression of the higher self by blending both feminine and masculine energies. Quetzalcoatl's avatars include the resplendent quetzal bird, which lives predominantly in the mountainous parts of Central America, and the rattlesnake. A snake shedding its skin is often considered a symbol of rebirth. Quetzalcoatl has a lot going on. Quetzalcoatl integrates spirit with matter, morphing light to fire to light in a flow of birth, death and rebirth. Many phoenix myths emulate Quetzalcoatl.

This dormant power, released with the union of the Sacred Feminine with the Sacred Masculine, is embodied, entwined and awaiting in each of us. Consciousness changes vibration, which changes relation, which brings revelation. As this unification occurs new potentials are created and activated. As mentioned, these energies lie within our DNA and without in the vibrational flow of the planet and universe. Quetzalcoatl demonstrates how to awaken this vital force, known as *coyopa* or lightning in the blood to the Maya. The awakening is not possible without the transformational consciousness and authentic expression we bring to the sacred space of sacred reciprocity, and in our daily life. Isn't it interesting that many Americans fear public speaking – expression – even more than they fear snakes – transformation?

Meeting Quetzalcoatl is a return to Serpent Spirit, an embrace of multi-dimensional realities and transformative energies. Quetzalcoatl is deeper medicine. The Feathered Serpent represents kinetic potential and activated power. The higher power not only is a Higher Power, but calls us to higher power by activating human potential through our connection with the vibrations of the planet. Activating it awakens us to greater potential and awareness through existing, but dormant, genetic codes or through the mutations brought about by the higher vibrations of consciousness. Ayni prepares the human mind, heart, spirit and body to channel these highly transformational energies through understanding that the universal connection with the web of life and the waters of consciousness is a prerequisite for spiritual activation.

Too many of us still assert that even though it has been proven countless times that the human body is electric, hence electromagnetic, it has no energy field of consequence. We are surrounded by subtle energies. We emit subtle energies. Yet science and medicine claim subtle energies are too subtle to influence subtle energies, and that from inner memory to planetary Schumann Resonances, none of these impact gene expression. To quote Spock again, "That is illogical." It is not only illogical; it is impossible. The cause and effect of subtle energies can be subtle and profound. Each and every human creation began with the subtlest of concepts: a thought. (At least I can't *imagine* any that didn't.) Yet, deniers deny we can make it rain, as did Wallace Black Elk and many others.

Connection is magic and magic spins the web of life. Once magical reciprocity is experienced, life stands to change measurably and immeasurably. With magic as a daily and constant affair, our path and perceptions change. We can choose to live in denial, and avoid the fringes of awe and bliss, or we can ascend Denali and attain a deeper sense of purpose, of being and becoming, of testing and trial and tribulation. That path is more difficult and much more entertaining. All it takes is a subtle change. You might find someone or something to guide or accompany you, but do something and the magic will always be yours. As that famous American mountaineer, Jim Whitaker, said, "If you aren't living on the edge, you are taking up too much space." That is not exactly how I felt that morning at the Grand Canyon, but he has a point. Let's take our sacred space to the edge.

My Little Chickadee

One spring morning at Winter Ouzel Creek, I looked to see if what I was watching was watching me. The day before, I looked at one of my bird field guidebooks to relearn some of the names and characteristics of migratory birds that were returning to Montana. The chickadee illustration caught my eye. It showed a chickadee on a very thin branch. It was not standing on the branch. Rather, it looked to me almost like a person who would use the hands to grab a bar and do a pull-up. The chickadee's feet were almost in the same hand position, as if the bird just pulled its head over a chin up bar. I looked at the illustration and thought, 'I don't think I've ever seen a chickadee do that.'

This particular morning a couple of chickadees flew into a willow right next to me. They were so close I didn't think they saw me, but they didn't fly away when I talked to them. One chickadee got into the "pull up position" on a branch over the water, exactly as I had seen in the field guide. I laughed a bit and thought if it couldn't fly when it let go, it would fall in. Then I pictured it letting go of the branch, and how far it would drop before it flew to another branch. And then the exact mental sequence I had just pictured happened. The chickadee let go of the branch, dropped maybe a foot or so, flapped its wings and flew to another branch. What struck me was that everything was as I had pictured. So, I imagine it to be an affirmation of whatever forces move men and chickadees and other song birds that the chickadee communicated with me by its behavior: 1) it flew right next to me, 2) it gripped a skinny branch in the way illustrated in a book I had seen the day before, and 3) confidently dropped off that branch above the water before it flew away, exactly as I had imagined. To me, it could not be clearer. I was being watched.

~~~~~~~~~~~~~~~~~~

Spiritual magic is not hocus pocus or sleight of hand, which imply illusion, delusion, trickery and distraction, entertaining as those can be. Knowledge, through experience, shapeshifts into wisdom. Spiritual wisdom leads to spiritual magic, and the practical use of either can yield even greater spiritual wisdom. The Earth and the unseen teach us through their wisdom by ushering us into the unknown, the abode of both magic and mystery. Magic is among the supreme movements. It is a reward and a way of life, and why and how the planet and other entities reciprocate with it when we trust enough to enter the unknown. Without magic we think we know the unknown and become bored with it. With magic, we know we don't know the unknown and need to consciously interact with it to appreciate it. Thus, when we offer our most heartfelt ayni, the planet gives us its best in return, a magic that teaches us to know what is by becoming more of what we already are – a vital and uniquely vibrating strand of the Imaginator/Imaginatrix matrix.

Magic is like love. We never know how, when or where it will show up. Most likely, we are the ones who must show up because it's already here. Magic is the essence of presence and sentience...of being present and aware. Magic is part of our co-created world. It is part of the Great Mysterious, which taught me I don't have to be careful what I ask for – if I ask for the right stuff in the right way.

Magic and knowledge are meant to be shared. They have not always been because some people who had magic and knowledge were feared and killed and discredited. Others were paid to use their knowledge improperly. That still happens. On the other hand, hidden knowledge fosters elitism and the self-importance of those who know it. It is difficult to say which is the bigger problem: ignorance or the improper use of knowledge. Wisdom can never be misused or faked. Wisdom cannot be manipulated for self-gratification. It isn't wisdom if it is; it may be only knowledge. That is how to tell the difference between the two. It is up to each of us to discern if a teacher is wise, knowledgeable or faking it, regardless of the form a teacher takes. If we crave wisdom, don't look for it from a teacher who is only knowledgeable. All of us can be Wisdom Keepers. All of us can be Wisdom Makers. To reciprocate
~~~~~~~~~~~~~~~~~~

with sacred offerings to things we witness and things that move us triggers our own wisdom.

As the heroic journey escapes from myth and enters our own lives, what is it we are being asked to do? I believe the answer lies in the ultimate purpose of the heroic journey, which is to bring something back in order to bring something forward. Although this journey is an individual quest, and the something we bring back is unique to each of us, there is also a common thread that is an evolutionary conduit necessary to each of us, and maybe needed more than ever. That something is sacred space, in which authentic reciprocity and magic wisdom abound. The heroic journey takes place within sacred space. So it is not just the purview of priests, mystics and saints anymore. Sacred space belongs to us all, especially in a world and time that often seem spinning out of control. The sacred space of within and without is the Holy Grail. Sacred space begins in the heart and the heroic journey brings it out. It's also the new treasure we can all bring back; the something we can all create, in the tradition of true and new alchemy. And whether we see it as half empty or half full or overflowing, how we fill it and with what we fill it is unique to us.

But sacred space is even more. Sacred space is the alchemist's philosopher's stone. It is also the crucible in which to bring order out of chaos and peace to the turbulence of much of the world today. As don Oscar says, "We must also daily cultivate the ability to embrace what is out of balance in the world, while simultaneously maintaining a state of equanimity, serenity and reverence within our hearts." Ayni reduces overwhelm brought about by imbalance. After we create peace and order out of chaos, we can begin to create a higher order out of order and who can say where that will lead?

There's another important thing we can do in sacred space: forgive. It doesn't matter who else forgives us if we do not forgive ourself. Sometimes I sit quietly in sacred space and forgive myself…for everything and anything. When I leave that space, all of that guilt and remorse are gone. What happened to it? Once guilt is released, its energy can change by the higher vibration of the sacred space. I also send negative feelings – guilt, anger, remorse – out my hands and into the earth where their energy can also be transformed. Without my attachment, which tends to lock them in place, the energies of lower vibrations can be more easily assimilated into something positive, which is what self-forgiveness and self-love are. The universe is forgiving and for giving. Or, if your prefer, the universe is forgetting and for getting.

Ceremonial reciprocity is like a kiss from a true lover. No two kisses are the same. Each is a heart-stopping, time-altering, endorphin-releasing treasure of lip connecting soul bonding love entwined in feathered serpent realization. So, I close my eyes and kiss back with all my heart. That is the essence of ayni to me, a whirlwind of heart-felt kisses I give back for everything I receive, leaving me with that ecstatic "I'm in love and I've lost my head" feeling. I hope such kisses make Kim[18] and Gawain and the Green Knight proud.

What better way to get even with the Universe than by getting right with the World with a kiss?

---

[18] Kim provided the endless bottle of Sun Dance aloe vera and the whirlwind of kisses when I sat at the creek in the Crazy Mountains.

Addendum

On Thanksgiving morning in 2016, my friend, George Karl, and his family loaded a twenty-four foot long horse trailer full of supplies. Then they drove from Bozeman, Montana to the Standing Rock Reservation in North Dakota, where water protectors were engaged in stopping the Dakota Access Pipeline. George is a gifted writer. While at Standing Rock he recorded much of his experience. Below is one episode. It powerfully encompasses concepts of ayni and connection.

"People have asked what it was like to be at Standing Rock. The experience was amazing in many ways. There were thousands of people there. There seemed to be no central organization, but everything was working well amongst the thousands who were there. Huge piles of clothing donations overflowed from tents. Many different kitchens cooked food for hundreds, prayer circles appeared at different times, songs were sung, medical supplies were sorted amongst medical tents, and flags from a hundred nations and places flew along a central way. Here is a piece I wrote from a morning along the Cannonball River.

A Singer by the River

He stood there with the frozen ground, with the crisp brown grass behind him, with the pastel colors of morning on the ice before him. He stood there listening to a Native man singing prayer songs across the river, listening to the man's drum, feeling the cold of the morning. He on one side of the Cannonball River, the singer on the other.

He felt the winter's cold morning, and remembered the night before when the stars were so bright overhead. It was a night for wearing three jackets, two pairs of socks and a wool hat. He stood with his son, looking up at Orion, his shoulders and head so bright, his belt and sword so straight and clear.

He had come with his son Peter, Veronika, Peter's girl friend, and Kathleen, Peter's mother to Standing Rock in support of the Protectors who believed that prayerful, non violent action could bring positive change. Kathleen had raised three thousand dollars, which filled the horse trailer with boxes, coolers and bags of much needed food and clothing.

They arrived late afternoon at Standing Rock to see thousands of people and hundreds of tents and teepees filling two camps where the

Cannonball and Missouri rivers meet at Turtle Island. Somehow he drove the trailer through the winding dirt ways between tents and kitchens, past a sacred fire, to Mona's Kitchen where they unloaded it in the half dark of flashlights and camp fires.

That night he asked his cousin Jewels, a young man with curly hair and a scruffy beard studying religion, "How do people pray during an action with police in front of them wearing riot gear and carrying weapons."

Jewels had been at Turtle Island the day before and stood before the police who held the ground high on a cliff above the Protectors, the police talking through megaphones and armed with rifles.

"How do you pray to bring change with non-violence, with fear before you? What was it like to pray? What did you hear in your mind? What do the elders say?"

Jewels shared his story with his family and friends, gathered in a white canvas tent, lit by flashlight, warmed with a wood fire in a small metal stove. Jewels talked about how there are many people in the world who do not distinguish between religion and living. It is in the West, said Jewels, that we separate religion and our lives.

The next morning, after Orion had lain below the morning horizon, he woke with his two dogs in the tent feeling the frost stiffen the nylon above his head. He was up early, went for a chilly walk, and stood by himself along the river.

He stood on the frozen ground, and listened to the morning prayer songs and the drum. The day before the earth had been soft, but last night's clear skies let the warmth escape, the cold descended to cover the earth, cover the water, with a frozen surface. The soft dawn light reflected beautiful pastels across the ice. The sounds of the Native songs came clearly. He watched the single First Nations singer with his drum, facing east, singing First Nation prayer songs in the morning. The singer was standing alone, and not alone at all. His songs traveled amongst thousands of people on both sides of the river.

He knew he too was in prayer, yet there was not a thought he heard nor a word pronounced in his mind, nor with his lips. He felt how prayer seemed to be a way of being, a way of being in life. He was in prayer, listening to prayer songs, aware of the world around, beneath him, in front of him. He asked for nothing, invoked nothing, spoke no word, no name, and felt Spirit with him as he stood next to the river.

The things he received had no word to describe them, yet they were full of substance. He closed his eyes, saw it all, heard it all, felt the cold morning air touch him all over.

The night before when looking at the stars, he and his son had heard a drum circle and First Nation songs sung in the darkness across the river. Many people beat the drum that night, and sang in the cold night air. Their songs lifted him upward in the night, and took him back to other prayer songs, other drums, other dancers who had danced in silence on hot dry earth, raising dust, adorned with sage, praying without saying anything at all."

Notes

Made in the USA
Middletown, DE
10 September 2020